PROJECT TEEN

Handmade Gifts Your Teen Will Actually Love

21 Projects to Sew

Melissa Mortenson

stashBOOKS.
an imprint of C&T Publishing

Text copyright © 2014 by Melissa Mortenson

Photography and Artwork copyright © 2014 by C&T Publishing, Inc.

Publisher: Amy Marson

Creative Director: Gailen Runge

Art Director: Kristy Zacharias

Editors: Lynn Koolish and Monica Gyulai

Technical Editors: Doreen Hazel and Mary Flynn

Cover/Book Designer: April Mostek

Page Layout Artist: Casey Dukes

Production Coordinator: Zinnia Heinzmann

Production Editor: Katie Van Amburg

Illustrator: Zinnia Heinzmann

Photo Assistant: Mary Peyton Peppo

Styled photography by Nissa Brehmer, unless otherwise noted; Instructional photography by Diane Pedersen, unless otherwise noted

Published by Stash Books, an imprint of C&T Publishing, Inc., P.O. Box 1456, Lafayette, CA 94549

Library of Congress Cataloging-in-Publication Data

Mortenson, Melissa, 1973-

 Project teen : handmade gifts your teen will actually love : 21 projects to sew / Melissa Mortenson.

  pages cm

 ISBN 978-1-60705-884-7 (soft cover)

 1. Machine sewing. 2. Gifts. I. Title.

 TT713.M67 2014

 745.59--dc23

                    2014002477

Printed in China

10 9 8 7 6 5 4 3 2 1

Dedication

I would like to dedicate this book to my family, especially my husband, Jeff, who so wisely asked me many years ago, "How do you know you can't do it if you haven't tried?"

Acknowledgments

Thank you to my kids, who are always so willing to cheer me on and let me work, and who give me a million ideas. You are truly the inspiration for the projects in this book.

Thank to you my mom, who, when I was a teenager, let me turn the basement into the messiest sewing room ever seen. Thank you for encouraging me to develop my talents when I was young.

Lastly, thank you to everyone at C&T Publishing, who worked so hard to make this book a reality. I am so grateful to you for taking a chance on me.

CONTENTS

In this book, I hope to inspire you. I want to inspire you to not just make quilts for that cute newborn baby. As babies grow into young adults, they can still use nice handmade gifts.

Teens Are Not Just Big Kids

Teens are forgetful, messy, emotional, and unpredictable. If you've ever had one, you know there is nothing quite like a teenager.

Perhaps the title on this page caught your eye? If you have a teen, you know that teens are not just small adults or big kids. They don't come with a set of operating instructions, even though I wish at times they did. This book won't help you navigate the emotional turmoil of the teen years. I'm sorry for that … you're in the wrong section of the bookstore. What it will do is offer a handful of projects for you to sew that are specifically designed with teens and tweens in mind.

Why sew for teenagers? Well, there are a lot of good reasons. For one, it's a great way to show your love for them. The teen years are full of turmoil, often characterized by tension between parents and teens. Teens need to feel loved just as much as little kids—maybe more. A handmade item is a great way to show that you love them.

Case in point: A few years ago I decided, like a crazy person, to make a quilt for each of my kids for Christmas. I've got three of them—kids, that is. Not being the best manager of time when it comes to large projects, I left more work for the last minute than I should have. I almost decided to just ditch the project, but I finished it.

My oldest daughter was sixteen at the time. I feared she might think it was the dumbest gift she received. But I will never forget the look on her face when she unwrapped the quilt. I don't think she was expecting it. There was love in that quilt, and she could tell. I had taken the time when designing the quilt to really think about *her*. What did she like? What were her favorite colors? I thought about her hobbies, the TV shows she liked, and the clothes she wore. I used all of these as clues when designing that quilt. Later that day I caught a glimpse of her curled up on the couch, wrapped in her new quilt. It was in that moment that I knew: Even though she was growing up, it was still important that I put effort into making things for her.

You too can sew for the teens in your life and discover that they might even like it! Just put thought into the project, and make sure it's really geared toward them.

I hope this book takes some of the fear out of sewing something a teen would like, and that it inspires you to make a special gift for that not-just-a-big-kid in your life.

TEENS AND TWEENS?

Choose Fabrics with Teens in Mind

Okay, let's start here. Teens are very trend conscious and picky. Most I've met are pretty definite about what they do and do not like. The fabric you choose can make or break your project. Here are a few tips to help get you started in making the perfect present for your teen:

- If your project is not a surprise, consider taking them shopping with you. Let them peruse the fabric store. Stand back and observe. What do they like? What are they gravitating to? Try not to offer too many suggestions at first; give them a few minutes to make choices.

- If shopping with them is not an option, think of their favorite things. Do they have any hobbies? What are their favorite colors? Not sure? Think of the outfit they were wearing the last time you saw them. Their choices in clothes will also give you a lot of ideas about the colors and patterns they like. Really take some time and think about it.

- Get inspiration from the retail world. Several retail stores specialize in teen clothing. Most of these stores are very loud—just get over it and go in! Notice the colors and the textures in the clothing and the displays. Is there a recurring motif? What is your teen's favorite place to shop for clothes? This might give you a great head start in finding fabric-selection inspiration.

- Teens love novelty fabrics. Have a soccer player? A hint of a soccer-themed fabric will go a long way toward eliciting a smile. I personally love to work with novelty fabrics. However, when working with these fabrics, it's best to use them sparingly. Start with a novelty fabric as your jumping-off point. After that, select more neutral pattern fabrics with a similar feel and color scheme. Doing this not only keeps your project from becoming overly busy, but it will also help the novelty fabric really stand out.

- If you need help picking a color scheme for a project, start with one fabric that you love and that has multiple colors in the design. Use those colors as your palette for your project. Try to stick to no more than three strong colors per project.

These are some of my favorite stores to visit for inspiration for teens:

Vera Bradley

PBteen (Pottery Barn Teen)

American Eagle Outfitters

Anthropologie

Johnnie B (by Boden)

These are some of my favorite fabric designers and manufacturers for teen-appropriate fabrics:

Echino

Riley Blake Designs

Amy Butler Design

Melody Miller

Alexander Henry Fabrics (great for novelty prints)

Birch Fabrics

Tula Pink

Lizzy House

PRECUT FABRICS

You can save time in cutting out your projects by using precut fabrics. In general, these bundles or stacks will come from a single collection from a single manufacturer or designer. Here's a quick guide to some popular precut fabric bundles:

Layer cake: stack of 40 or 42 coordinating 10″ × 10″ squares (I frequently buy white-only layer cakes for use in quilt backgrounds.)

Charm pack: stack of 25–40 coordinating 5″ × 5″ squares (Some manufacturers use 6″ × 6″ squares in their charm packs. Double-check the label before you purchase.)

Jelly roll: roll of 40 coordinating fabric strips, 2½″ × width of fabric (These come in a variety of names, including Design Roll and Rolie Polie. They are great to use for borders or sashing in the quilt projects.)

There's one other precut that you can purchase in bundles or individually. Instead of the usual quarter yard that is cut 9″ × width of fabric, a **fat quarter** is cut 18″ × 22″. Fat quarters provide lots of variety in print fabrics and less wasted fabric. You'll see them specified in many of the projects.

TIP *The projects in this book provide a great way to use appropriate fabrics from your stash. Solids and stripes, for example, will work well with the modern prints that are used as primary fabrics in many of the projects.*

BASIC TOOLS
AND GOOD SEWING PRACTICES

Even though the projects in this book are varied, many of the tools and techniques used for making them are shared. Here are some supplies you'll want to have on hand as you make the bags, cases, quilts, and other projects presented in this book. Specific materials are listed with each project.

Sewing Machine Feet

Did your sewing machine come with a bunch of extra feet? Do you feel like you don't have the faintest idea what some of them do? Well, it's time to learn! Using special feet correctly can save you both time and frustration. Here are some of the feet that I use over and over again. Some don't typically come with a sewing machine, but they are worth buying to make repeated techniques easier.

A Edge-stitch foot: A bar underneath the foot allows you to follow the shape of fabric, such as a curve or an appliqué, and sew close to the edge.

B Nonstick foot: A must if you sew with laminated or coated fabrics. The bottom is coated in Teflon so the foot doesn't stick to the fabric as it's being stitched.

C Zipper foot: A must for attaching zippers.

D Piping foot: A foot with a groove under the bottom that allows piping to smoothly pass underneath—a lifesaver if you work with a lot of piping.

E Walking foot: You might think that a walking foot is only used for machine quilting, but I'm here to tell you that is not the case. A walking foot helps feed fabrics through the machine easily and evenly. I use it on everything from tote bags to quilt bindings. Some machines have a built-in walking foot.

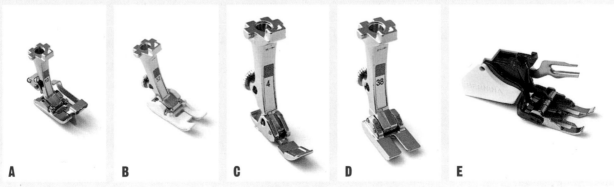

A   B   C   D   E

Sewing machine feet

Tools I Love

A Sewing machine: There are loads of great sewing machines on the market right now. If you're looking for a new machine, start at your local sewing machine shop, where dealers can help you identify which features you need and give you the opportunity to test drive a few machines to see what you like. They can also service machines and answer questions after your purchase. I sew with a Bernina 710, which sews through multiple layers of fabric with ease and is large enough for me to feed a big quilt through without much struggle. It also has a built-in walking foot, which I adore!

B Sharp scissors: Invest in a good pair and cut only fabric with them! I have a large pair for cutting fabric and a small pair that I use to clip threads and to cut out appliqué shapes.

C Good thread: Cheap thread can contain extra oils and fibers that you don't want running through your machine. High-quality thread will minimize lint buildup in your machine and give you a cleaner look on your finished projects. My favorite is Aurifil.

I like to use 100% cotton thread for quilting projects and 100% polyester thread for bags and items that will have a lot of wear and tear.

D Seam ripper: Get one that is an "all-in-one" tool that includes a seam ripper and a few other features. I like Alex Anderson's 4-in-1 Essential Sewing Tool from C&T Publishing—it includes a seam ripper, a

A My sewing space

stiletto, a presser, and a tube turner with a pointed wood end (great for pushing out corners).

E Pressing ham: A pressing ham will help you press seams that are difficult to get to. This comes in especially handy when constructing handbags.

F Sleeve board: Like the pressing ham, this will come in handy when pressing hard-to-get-to seams.

G Good-quality iron: You want an iron that has lots of steam and gets very hot! You'll be amazed what a difference pressing a project will make. Don't rush when pressing—take the time to press after each step. The extra effort will show in your finished project.

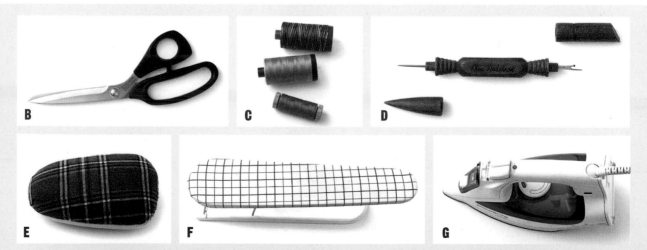

B **C** **D** **E** **F** **G**

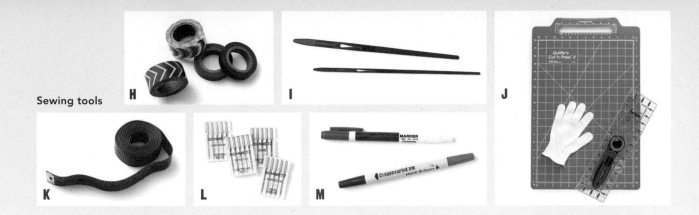

Sewing tools

H Washi tape: Are you surprised to see this one on the list? Besides being cute and useful for crafting, this decorative Japanese tape is great for marking a seam allowance on your sewing machine because it's removable. You can also use blue painter's tape if you don't have washi tape.

I Turning tools: These tools will make quick work of any tube you have to turn, and the wood sticks that come with them are great for poking out corners.

J Quilt rulers, rotary cutter, and cut glove: These make quick work of cutting out fabric, but that rotary cutter is sharp! Wear a cut glove to protect your non-cutting hand (trust me—I learned this one the hard way).

K Measuring tape: A must for any sewing basket.

L Extra needles: Certain sewing machine needles work best for different types of fabrics. Make sure that you are using the correct one for your fabric or thread. Did you know that you should change your needle with almost every project? A dull needle can cause many problems—I also learned this one the hard way. Buy them in bulk so you always have fresh ones at the ready.

M Fabric-safe marking pen: Sometimes it's just easier to write on your fabric. I can't sew without these anymore. Depending on the brand, the ink will disappear with water, time, or heat. To be safe, always test your pen on a scrap piece of fabric first, and then mark away!

TROUBLESHOOTING MACHINE PROBLEMS

If your machine suddenly starts behaving oddly or producing poor-quality stitches, try the following:

- If the machine is computerized, turn it off and back on again.

- Rethread the machine completely, including the bobbin.

- Change the sewing machine needle.

- Check the fabric setting or the tension. Are you sewing on woven light fabric and using a woven heavy fabric setting?

- Make sure you are using the right needle for the fabric. If you are sewing a knit, you need a stretch needle. A jeans needle will help with sewing heavy-duty fabrics.

- Check to see if there is an excessive amount of lint under the bobbin. If so, clean it out.

A Few Other Tips

1 Press your seams often. There is a difference between pressing and ironing. To press, raise and lower the iron over your fabric, but do not make any back-and-forth motions, which can distort the fabric. This is especially important when piecing quilts.

2 Know the seam allowance for a project and stick to it consistently. I find it helpful to use washi tape (or painter's tape) to mark a seam allowance on my sewing machine.

3 Clip corners and curves and grade seams.

4 Read all of the directions for a project before you start. This will help prevent silly mistakes.

TECHNIQUES

Appliqué

The projects in this book feature appliqué using paper-backed fusible web. The web sticks to fabric when ironed and acts like glue between two pieces of fabric. It has paper on one side so that you can iron the first sticky side onto a piece of fabric and then peel the paper backing off and iron another fabric to the back. The paper backing is also very convenient to use for drawing and tracing appliqué images.

USING COMPUTER FONTS AS APPLIQUÉ PATTERNS

If you have a computer and a few attractive fonts, you can have a lot of fun designing your own appliqué patterns using a word-processing or graphics program. I use Microsoft Word or Adobe Photoshop for most of my appliqué patterns.

Make the Pattern

1 Type the word you want into your computer program.

2 Pick a font that you like. Some fun and free ones to try are Pacifico, Bebas, Museo Slab, and ChunkFive (or Chunk Five Ex). Wisdom Script, a thick script style ideal for appliqué, is available for a nominal fee. Georgia and Arial in Microsoft Word are also good choices. (Refer to fonts in Supplies and Resources, page 127.)

3 Make the word the size you want for your appliqué. The size will be measured in points or picas, but it's more helpful to use a standard 8½″ × 11″ paper as a guide for making the appropriate size. Many computer programs also have on-screen rulers. For large words, select the "landscape" orientation on the document setting.

4 Print and check the size of the letters. **A**

Make the Appliqué

1 To use paper-backed fusible web, you'll need to *reverse* the word. You can use a lightbox or bright window and trace the word onto the *paper* side of the paper-backed fusible web. After you trace it, the word will be reversed. Alternatively, reverse the image in a photo program before printing it out or check your printer options—many have an option to mirror or reverse what is to be printed. **B**

2 Loosely cut out the word from the paper-backed fusible web.

3 With the paper side up, iron the fusible onto the wrong side of the appliqué fabric. Follow the manufacturer's instructions for pressing. **C**

4 Precisely cut out each letter along the traced lines on the paper backing. **D**

5 Peel off the paper backing. Place the letters in position, web side down. Press to fuse in place.

A Print word in selected font.

B Trace appliqué on paper-backed fusible web.

C Iron fusible onto fabric.

D Appliqué completed and ready for sewing

APPLIQUÉ STITCHING

For my appliqués I like to use paper-backed fusible web so that the appliqué sticks well. However, fusible web alone might peel off over time, so it's important to stitch the edges of an appliqué. This both secures it and gives it a nice, finished look. To stitch down the appliqué, there are two stitches I like most—straight and blanket.

Straight Stitch

1 After the appliqué is fused in place, use a straight stitch to stitch just inside the raw edge of the appliqué, being careful not to stitch beyond the edge. An edge stitching foot will help keep stitching lines consistent. **A**

2 When you get to a corner, put the needle down, raise the sewing machine foot, and pivot. Begin sewing again.

3 For curves you may need to do several small pivots to get a clean look.

Blanket Stitch

To use this method, you need a machine with decorative stitches.

1 Find the blanket stitch setting on your machine. It will look like this: |_|_|_|_| .

2 Test the stitch on a scrap to determine where the stitches fall. Aim to have the vertical stitches along the edge of the appliqué and the horizontal stitches landing just inside. **B**

3 Begin stitching the fused appliqué. When you get to a corner, put the needle down and pivot. Try to make sure that you are at the appropriate point in the stitch pattern when you pivot. In other words, pay attention to which direction the needle will go next before you pivot.

4 You may need to pivot several times for curves.

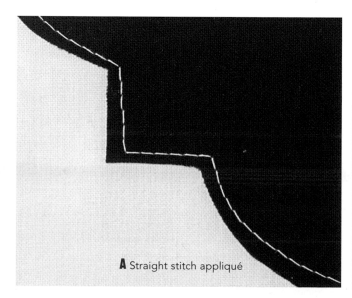

A Straight stitch appliqué

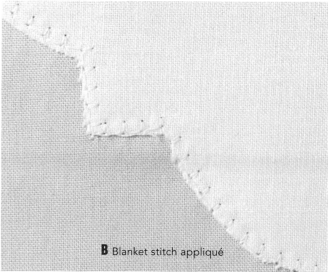

B Blanket stitch appliqué

Printing on Fabric

If you want to print on fabric, you will need to purchase fabric specifically made for printing with an inkjet printer. These fabrics come backed with paper so that the fabric can pass easily through a printer. After printing, you remove the paper. There are two types of printable fabric readily available: fusible and nonfusible. For the projects in this book, use nonfusible printable fabric. Fusible printable fabric has a coating on the back so that it can be ironed onto another surface.

Lesley Riley's TAP Transfer Artist Paper (TAP) is another good option for printing text and images on fabric, and it allows you to choose the kind of fabric you want to use. TAP is available in quilt shops, craft stores, and online (see Supplies and Resources, page 127).

live a COLORFUL life

Image printed on fabric

PRINT IMAGE ON FABRIC

1 Open the image you want to print. Often it will be a PDF file.

2 Load a sheet of non-fusible printable fabric into your printer. Make sure you know which side needs to be face up for your particular printer. You want to print on the fabric, not the backing!

3 Choose a "normal" print setting (using "photo" or "best" may leave too much ink on the fabric). Leave the paper type and size as standard. After printing, allow the fabric to dry for at least 10 minutes.

4 Peel off the paper backing.

5 Give the fabric a good pressing to set the ink and shrink the fabric. Do *not* cut out the fabric until after you do this step. If you cut before ironing, the final piece will not be the correct size.

6 Sew as you would with regular fabric.

Important!

If you are not using your own photos or images, get permission from the image creator to use the image in your project.

A FEW TIPS

- Before going to all the trouble of making a quilt out of printed fabric, make a test piece first. Check to see if the color holds up after the piece is washed. Some printed fabrics may fade if exposed to direct sunlight for an extended period.

- Read the directions on the package. Different manufacturers may have different techniques to set the ink. Don't skip this step. Once I didn't run cold water over my printed image as was called for on the package. When I washed the item, the ink bled all over my finished project. It was a mess! Take the time to read all the directions.

- I have played around with many printable fabrics. I really like Regular Cotton Inkjet Fabric Sheets by Electric Quilt.

- Images (such as photographs) print better if you first increase the color saturation using a photo-editing program.

Distressing Duck Cloth and Canvas

A few years ago, I searched unsuccessfully for sun-bleached, colored canvas. I decided to try for a similar look by distressing duck cloth. To my surprise, it worked like a charm. At the end of the process, that stiff, unbendable fabric had become buttery soft. You can distress canvas in the same way, but duck cloth is more widely available in a variety of fun and bright colors at most big-box fabric stores.

DISTRESS THE DUCK CLOTH

1 Wash the fabric in hot water using both detergent and liquid fabric softener.

2 Tumble dry the fabric at the highest heat setting and with a softener sheet.

3 Repeat Steps 1 and 2 until the fabric has a soft feel and all stiffness is removed. This usually takes me 3 wash cycles.

4 Hang the fabric in the sun to fade it a bit more if you want it lighter. Duck cloth is not colorfast, so it shouldn't be forgotten outside, but an afternoon in the sun will lighten it up a bit. And don't iron the duck cloth before hanging it up—the wrinkles will give the fabric extra texture as it lightens. The fabric will continue to fade if you wash it.

Duck cloth

Distressed duck cloth

Working with Piping

Piping is a narrow strip of fabric sewn around a cord or string. When inserted into a sewn seam, the side with the cording shows, and the side with the raw fabric is hidden away, just like the other raw edges of the seam. Piping gives sewn items a professional, finished appearance. I love prepackaged piping because it comes in loads of colors and is inexpensive, but you can make your own too.

A special cording or piping foot gives a nicer result and will probably save you a lot of aggravation. But if you don't have one, the zipper foot that came with your machine can be used. Run the zipper foot as close to the piping as possible, with the needle as far over to the side as possible. The goal is to sew as close as you can to the cording so that you get a clean finish on the right side.

1 Place piping on the right side of your fabric, with the raw edge of the piping even with the raw edge of the fabric.

2 Attach a cording foot to your sewing machine. Place the piping under the presser foot so that the bulk of the cording is under the groove in the bottom of your presser foot. Adjust the needle to the left or right so that the needle sews right next to the edge of the cording. **A**

3 If you need to turn a corner, stop ¼″ before reaching the corner. Clip through the fabric portion of the piping toward the cording, being careful not to cut through the stitching and into the cord. The piping tube will now be able to turn at a 90° angle. Pivot your fabric and turn the piping to begin sewing again along the next edge. **B**

TIP *Joining the ends of piping for a neat finish within a seam can be a bit tricky. For a simple method refer to my blog at polkadotchair.com > My Tutorials > Sewing Tutorials > Sewing Lesson: How to Make and Sew Piping.*

4 To enclose the piping in a seam, take a second piece of fabric and place it on top of the fabric onto which you just sewed the piping, raw edges together. For a pillow, place the pillow back on top of the pillow front, right sides together, with the piping sandwiched between them.

5 Flip the fabric over and pin from the side on which you can see the stitching line you created when attaching the piping. Sew the 2 pieces of fabric together on this line—or just inside it, closer to the cord. This will ensure that your piping, and not the stitching, shows correctly when the piece is turned right side out. **C & D**

A Piping under foot of sewing machine

B Piping going around corner

C Piping sandwiched between 2 pieces of fabric

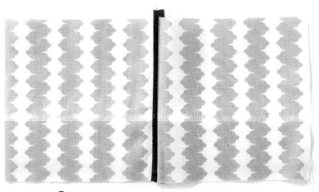

D Completed piece with piping inserted

Constructing a Basic Zip Pouch

I adore making zip pouches! They seem a bit confusing at first, but once you sew one you will be hooked too.

MAKE ZIPPER TABS

This technique works only for polyester, not metal, zippers.

1 Fold a 2″ × 2″ piece of fabric in half, wrong sides together. Press.

2 Unfold and press the 2 raw edges to the fold in the center. Leave a scant ¹⁄₁₆″ between the 2 folds. Press. Refold in the center and press again. The zipper tab will now measure ½″ × 2″.

3 Repeat Steps 1 and 2 to make a total of 2 tabs.

4 Pin each end of the zipper inside a folded zipper tab. The raw end of the zipper should be touching the center fold of the tab.

5 Stitch the zipper tab to the zipper. Trim the tab to match the sides of the zipper tape. The zipper tab is now the new zipper stop, so that the zipper won't come apart at the ends.

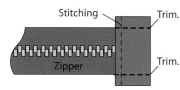

Stitching ——— Trim.

Zipper

Trim.

Zipper tab attached to zipper

TIP *Did you know that you can cut polyester zippers to any size that you need? I like to start with zippers that are longer than I need and then cut them down to the right size. If you only have a 12″ zipper on hand, and you need a 9″, you can just trim off the extra! Just remember that when you trim off the zipper stops, you have to add zipper tabs (see Make Zipper Tabs, above) to secure the ends of the zipper.*

TIP *Adding tabs to a zipper gives it a finished appearance. By acting as new zipper stops, the tabs also allow you to cut a polyester zipper to any length.*

ASSEMBLE THE POUCH

1 Pin the right side of the zipper to the right side of the pouch outside piece. If you have added extension tabs to the zipper because a project calls for them, the zipper will be ½″ shorter on each side than the pouch outside pieces. Simply center the zipper on the pouch outside piece. If the zipper does not have tabs, the zipper is the same length as the pouch outside piece.

2 Pin the right side of the pouch lining piece to the wrong side of the zipper.

3 Using a zipper foot, stitch the zipper to both the pouch outside and the pouch lining pieces. **A**

4 Repeat Steps 1–3 to attach the other pouch outside and pouch lining pieces to the other side of the zipper.

5 Press the seams of the pouch away from the zipper. Topstitch along both sides of the zipper. **B**

6 Unzip the zipper.

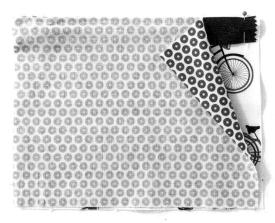

A Stitch zipper to pouch front and lining pieces.

7 Pin the 2 pouch outside pieces together, with right sides facing. Repeat for the 2 pouch lining pieces. Pin the zipper seam allowances toward the pouch lining pieces.

8 Stitch around the perimeter of the pouch, leaving a 3″ opening in the bottom of the pouch lining section. **C**

9 Clip the corners and turn the pouch right side out. Slipstitch the opening in the pouch lining closed.

Quiltmaking Basics

BATTING

The type of batting to use is a personal decision. Cut batting 6″–8″ longer and wider than your quilt top. Join two pieces if necessary. Note that your batting choice will determine how far apart the quilting lines can be.

LAYERING

Spread the backing wrong side up and tape the edges down with masking tape. (If you are working on carpet, you can use T-pins to secure the backing to the carpet.) Center the batting on top, smoothing out any folds. Place the quilt top right side up on top of the batting and backing, making sure it is centered.

BASTING

Basting keeps the quilt "sandwich" layers from shifting while you are quilting.

If you plan to machine quilt, pin baste the quilt layers together with safety pins placed about 3″–4″ apart. Begin basting in the center and move toward the edges, first in vertical and then in horizontal rows. Try not to pin directly on the intended quilting lines.

If you plan to hand quilt, baste the layers together with thread using a long needle and light-colored thread. Knot an end of the thread. Using stitches approximately the length of the needle, begin in the center and move out toward the edges in vertical and horizontal rows approximately 4″ apart. Add 2 diagonal rows of basting.

QUILTING

1 Quilting enhances the pieced or appliquéd design of the quilt. You may choose to quilt in-the-ditch, echo the appliqué motifs, use patterns from quilting design books, or do your own free-motion quilting. Remember to check your batting manufacturer's recommendations for minimum distance between quilting lines.

2 Trim excess backing and batting even with the edges of the quilt top.

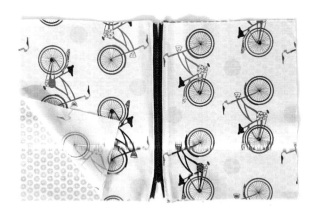

B Topstitch both sides of zipper.

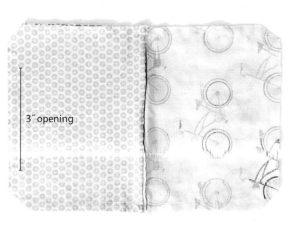

3″ opening

C Stitch perimeter, leaving 3″ opening.

BINDING

Make the Binding

1 Cut the binding strips as directed in each project and piece them together with ¼˝ straight seams to make a continuous binding strip. Press the seams open.

2 Press the entire strip in half lengthwise with wrong sides together.

Attach the Binding

1 With raw edges even, pin the binding to the right side of the quilt a few inches away from a corner, and leave the first few inches of the binding unattached. Start sewing, using a ¼˝ seam allowance. Stop ¼˝ before you get to a corner. **A**

2 Backstitch and then remove the fabric from the machine.

3 Insert a straight pin at a 45° angle from the corner.

4 Flip up the binding. **B**

5 Flip the binding back down, lining up the fold with top edge of the fabric. Begin stitching again. **C**

Note

For the blanket projects in this book, the binding is attached to the wrong side of the blanket first, but the same method applies.

Finish the Binding Ends

1 After stitching around the quilt, fold under the beginning tail of the binding strip ¼˝ so that the raw edge will be inside the binding after it is turned to the back of the quilt.

2 Place the end tail of the binding strip over the beginning folded end. Continue to attach the binding and stitch slightly beyond the starting stitches. Trim the excess binding.

3 Fold the binding over the raw edges to the quilt back and hand stitch, mitering the corners.

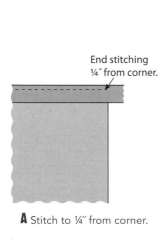

A Stitch to ¼˝ from corner.

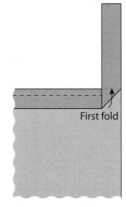

B First fold for miter

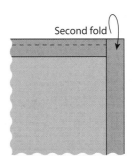

C Second fold alignment

THINGS THAT TRAVEL

Teens are constantly on the go. It seems at times that they never stop moving! They jump from school, to studying, to practice, and then they return home only to rise early the next day and do it all over again. This get-up-and-go lifestyle creates great opportunities to sew some fun carriers and cases. If you're looking for an idea for a gift for a teen, why not start with something that travels along with them?

Swim Bag

FINISHED SIZES: *Swim bag:* 14˝ high × 17˝ wide × 4˝ deep
Wristlet: 5˝ × 9˝ • *Wet pouch:* 9˝ × 12˝

This swim bag is roomy enough for a towel and sunscreen, but not too large to carry comfortably. It also includes a wristlet for a quick trip to buy a treat. For one last touch, make a wet pouch from clear vinyl. No more forgetting about a wet swimsuit!

Materials

SWIM BAG

- **Fabric A for bag outside:** ¾ yard decor-weight cotton

- **Fabric B for bag lining:** ¾ yard decor-weight cotton

- **Fabric C for inside pocket, reinforcement panel, and appliqué:** 2 fat quarters (18″ × 22″ each)

- **Fusible fleece:** ¾ yard, 44″ wide

- **Cotton rope for handles:** 2 yards

- **Plastic canvas:** 1 piece 4″ × 13″

- **4 grommets:** 1″ diameter

- **Leash clasp** (often used on purses and handbags)

WRISTLET

- **Fabric D for wristlet outside:** 1 fat quarter (18″ × 22″)

- **Fabric E for wristlet lining:** 1 fat quarter (18″ × 22″)

- **Iron-on vinyl:** 12″ × 20″ piece

- **Heavyweight nonfusible interfacing (such as Stitch*n*Sew Non-Woven Cut-Away Medium Weight Soft):** ½ yard, 20″ wide

- **Ribbon:** ⅓ yard, ⅜″ wide

- **Zipper:** 12″ all-purpose polyester

- **D-ring:** 1, size ½″

WET POUCH

- **Clear vinyl (quilter's vinyl or upholstery vinyl):** at least 16″ × 36″

- **Extra-wide double-fold bias tape:** 3 yards (1 package)

- **Cover button (Dritz):** 1, size ⅞″

Cutting

SWIM BAG

From decor-weight fabric

- Fabric A for bag outside:
  2 pieces 15″ × 18″
  1 piece 5″ × 14″ for bottom

- Fabric B for bag lining:
  2 pieces 15″ × 18″
  1 piece 5″ × 14″ for bottom

From fat quarters

- Fabric C:
  2 pieces 4½″ × 14″ for bottom reinforcement
  1 piece 18″ × 22″ for inside pocket
  1 piece 8″ × 10″ for appliqué

From fusible fleece

  2 pieces 15″ × 18″
  1 piece 5″ × 14″

WRISTLET

From fat quarters

- Fabric D for wristlet outside:
  2 pieces 6″ × 10″

- Fabric E for wristlet lining:
  2 pieces 6″ × 10″
  2 pieces 2″ × 2″ for zipper tabs

From iron-on vinyl

  2 pieces 6″ × 10″

From heavyweight nonfusible interfacing

  2 pieces 6″ × 10″

WET POUCH

From clear vinyl

  2 pieces 9″ × 12″
  1 piece 6″ × 12″ for flap

Make the Swim Bag

Seam allowances are ½″ unless otherwise noted.

MAKE THE OUTSIDE OF THE BAG

1 Make the "swim" appliqué using the techniques in Using Computer Fonts as Appliqué Patterns (page 10). I used the font Wisdom Script. The appliqué should be 10½″ long when printed.

2 Place the appliqué on the bag front piece 4½″ up from the bottom and 1″ in from the right edge, right side facing up. Fuse in place.

3 Sew down the appliqué, following the instructions in Appliqué Stitching (page 12). When stitching down words with many curves and pivots, you can sew close to the edge with an edge-stitch foot or just stitch down the center of the letters. The second approach may be easier with the "swim" appliqué, which has many curves. **A**

4 Iron fusible fleece to the wrong side of the 2 bag outside pieces 15″ × 18″.

5 Iron fusible fleece to the wrong side of the bag bottom outside piece 5″ × 14″.

A "Swim" appliqué

6 Stitch the 2 bag outside pieces together at the 15″ side seams. Press the seams open.

7 Topstitch along both sides of the bag side seams. **B**

8 Mark the center of the short sides of the bag bottom piece 5″ × 14″. **C**

9 Match the centers of the bag bottom piece with the bag side seams, right sides together. Pin the bag bottom in place, clipping the bag to, but not through, the seamlines at the corners. **D**

10 To stitch the bag bottom in place, start with the 2 long sides. Then stitch the 2 short sides.

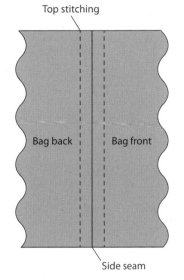

Top stitching

Bag back | Bag front

Side seam

B Topstitch.

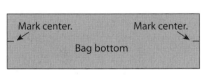

Mark center. | Mark center.

Bag bottom

C Mark centers on bottom piece.

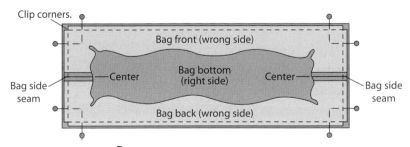

Clip corners.

Bag front (wrong side)

Bag side seam

Center | Bag bottom (right side) | Center

Bag side seam

Bag back (wrong side)

D Join bag bottom and bag outside.

MAKE THE BAG LINING AND INSIDE POCKET

1 Fold the fat quarter (18″ × 22″) for the pocket in half parallel to the 18″ edge. Press. The piece should now be 11″ tall × 18″ wide.

2 Topstitch along the fold.

3 Pin the pocket to a bag lining piece, right sides facing up, and the topstitched fold at the top. Baste it in place on the sides.

4 Find the center of the pocket and stitch along the midline, dividing the pocket in half.

5 Cut a 10″ piece of ribbon. Loop the ribbon through the leash clasp and pin it to the wrong side of the bag lining. Stitch the ribbon in place close to the top of the pocket. **E**

6 Assemble the remainder of the bag lining by repeating Steps 6–10 of Make the Outside of the Bag (page 23). Omit the side seam top stitching.

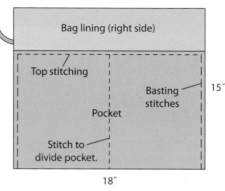

E Inside pocket

ASSEMBLE THE SWIM BAG

1 Press under the top edge ½″ on both the bag and the bag lining.

2 With wrong sides together, slip the bag lining into the bag, matching the centers and the side seams. Pin well.

3 Using a walking foot, topstitch around the bag top ¼″ down from the bag top.

ATTACH THE GROMMETS

1 Measure 4″ in from the side seam of the bag and 1″ down from the bag top and mark. Repeat for all 4 grommets—2 on the bag front and 2 on the bag back. **F**

2 Attach the grommets to the bag according to the manufacturer's instructions.

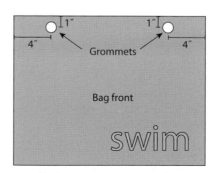

F Mark grommet placement.

FINISH THE BAG

1 Cut the cotton rope for the handles to the desired length.

2 Pass the rope through the grommets and tie to secure. If necessary, place a couple of hand stitches through the knot to ensure that it holds.

3 Stitch the 2 bag bottom reinforcement pieces 4½″ × 14″ together, right sides facing, leaving 1 of the 4″ sides open. Turn right side out and press.

4 Insert the plastic canvas piece 4″ × 13″ into the bag bottom reinforcement piece. Fold under raw edges and slipstitch the opening closed.

5 Place the bag bottom reinforcement piece into the bottom of the bag.

Make the Wristlet

All sewing on the wristlet is done with a nonstick foot. All seam allowances are ¼˝ unless otherwise noted.

1 Iron vinyl onto the 2 wristlet outside pieces 6˝ × 10˝, following the manufacturer's instructions. Save the paper backing from the vinyl to use as a "pressing cloth" later.

2 Using a CD or a similar size circular shape as a template, round off the 2 bottom corners of the wristlet front and back pieces.

3 Baste the heavyweight interfacing onto the wrong side of the 2 wristlet lining pieces 6˝ × 10˝.

4 Round the corners of the wristlet lining pieces (use the front pieces as a guide).

5 Feed a 4˝-long piece of ribbon through the D-ring. Fold the ribbon in half. Pin the ribbon to the wristlet front piece 2˝ down from top left corner. Stitch in place.

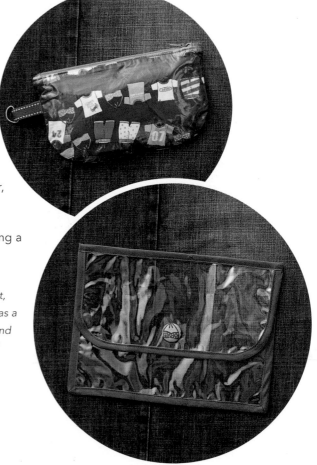

Round corners.

ASSEMBLE THE WRISTLET

1 Trim the 12˝ zipper down to 9˝ (trim off both zipper stops).

2 Make 2 zipper tabs and attach them to the ends of the zipper, following the instructions for Make Zipper Tabs (page 16).

3 To complete the pouch, follow the instructions for Constructing a Basic Zip Pouch (page 16).

TIP *If your wristlet is in need of pressing after you turn it right side out, you can use the paper backing that you peeled off the vinyl fabric as a "pressing cloth." Place the shiny side of the backing against the vinyl and press on a low setting. Do not put the iron directly on the vinyl-coated fabric because it will melt!*

Make the Wet Pouch

1 Cut a notch out of a 9″ × 12″ clear vinyl piece. Mark 1″ in from each side and 1″ down from the top. You can use tape or a thin-line pen to mark the cutting lines. Refer to the notch cutout diagram for placement. **A**

2 Place the 2 vinyl 9″ × 12″ pieces on top of each other. Use binding clips to hold the 2 pieces together.

3 Unfold your double-fold bias tape. Beginning at the top right corner of the wet pouch, align the raw edge of the right side of the bias tape and the edge of the vinyl pouch, right sides together. Stitch in place with a ¼″ seam allowance.

4 When you get to a corner, follow the steps for Attach the Binding (page 18). **B**

5 After sewing the bias tape to the pouch, refold the tape so that it covers the raw edge of the pouch (and assumes its original shape). Stitch the bias tape in place close to the fold of the bias tape, stitching through all layers of the pouch and the bias tape. Trim ends of bias tape even with pouch.

6 Round the 2 corners of the bottom of the bag flap.

7 Follow Steps 3–5 to apply bias tape to the bag flap. Do not apply the bias tape to the top edge of flap.

8 Clip the flap to the wet pouch along the top edge. Cut a piece of double-fold bias tape ½″ longer than the top edge of the flap. Turn under each end of this piece of bias tape ¼″, so that there are no raw edges. Clip the bias tape to the top of the bag/flap unit, following Steps 3–5. **C**

FINISH THE WET POUCH

1 Cut a 1½″ slit in the center of the flap 1½″ up from the bottom of the flap.

2 Cover the button with fabric from your swim bag or wristlet, following the button manufacturer's instructions.

3 Stitch the button to the wet pouch so that it lines up with the slit you cut in the bag flap.

TIP *I find it best to use binding clips rather than pins when working with laminate and vinyl fabrics. Pins will leave holes in the vinyl.*

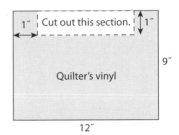

A Notch cutout

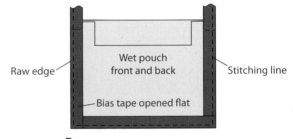

B Sew open bias tape to pouch.

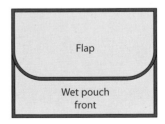

C Attach flap to bag.

Hello Bag

FINISHED SIZE: 13″ × 14″

My girls love bags that they can carry across their body. This one features an adjustable strap and an outer zip pocket for quick access to important things (such as lip gloss, of course!).

Materials

- **Fabric A for bag outside bottom:** ½ yard
- **Fabric B for bag outside and straps:** 1 yard
- **Fabric C for bag outside:** ⅓ yard
- **Fabric for lining:** 1½ yards
- **Décor Bond fusible interfacing (firm):** ½ yard, 44″ wide
- **Canvas:** ½ yard
- **Zippers:** 18″ all-purpose for outside pocket, 14″ all-purpose for inside pocket
- **Buttons:** 3, 1″ diameter
- **Bag ring:** 2″ rectangular

Cutting

From fabric A

- 2 pieces from the Bag Bottom pattern (page 36) for bag outside bottom

  (Note that this pattern is cut on folded fabric.)

From fabric B

- 2 pieces 5½″ × 14″ for bag outside
- 4 pieces 2″ × 13″ for inside zipper placket
- 2 pieces 2½″ × 40″ for bag strap
- 2 pieces 2½″ × 18″ for bag strap

From fabric C

- 2 pieces 3½″ × 14″ for bag outside

From canvas

- 1 piece 3½″ × 14″ for interfacing

From lining fabric

- 2 pieces 4″ × 14″ for bag lining
- 2 pieces 2″ × 2″ for zipper tabs
- 1 piece 9½″ × 14″ for outer pocket lining
- 1 piece 2″ × 14″ for outer pocket lining
- 1 piece 8″ × 14″ for outer pocket lining

From fusible interfacing

- 1 piece 2½″ × 18″ for bag strap
- 1 piece 2½″ × 40″ for bag strap

Additional bag lining and canvas pieces will be cut in the following steps.

Make the Hello Bag

All seam allowances are ½˝ unless otherwise noted.

MAKE THE OUTSIDE BAG FRONT

1 Sew the bag bottom piece (fabric A) to the bag outside piece 5½˝ × 14˝ (fabric B) along the 14˝ edge, right sides together. This piece is now referred to as the *sewn bag bottom*.

2 Press the seam open.

3 Cut a piece of canvas, using the sewn bag bottom as a pattern. **A**

4 Baste the canvas to the wrong side of the sewn bag bottom along the top edge.

5 Topstitch along both sides of the seam between the bag bottom and the bag outside piece. **B**

ATTACH THE OUTSIDE ZIPPER

1 Pin an edge of the 18˝ zipper to the top edge of the sewn bag bottom, right sides facing. The zipper will be much longer than this piece; for now, just center the sewn bag piece on the zipper. Baste together. **C**

2 Pin a long edge of the outer pocket lining 8˝ × 14˝, wrong side facing up, to the zipper. The zipper is now sandwiched between the sewn bag bottom and the outer pocket lining, right sides facing. **D**

3 Use a zipper foot to stitch through all the layers. Press the seams away from the zipper.

4 Baste the canvas piece 3½˝ × 14˝ to the wrong side of a bag outside piece 3½˝ × 14˝ (fabric C) on the long edges.

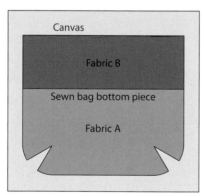

A Canvas sewn bag bottom

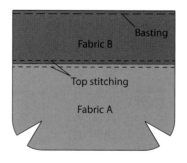

B

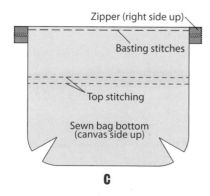

C

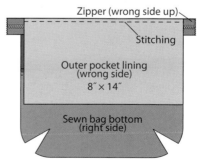

D Attach zipper to bag and outer pocket lining.

5 Pin the other edge of the zipper to a 14″ edge of the canvas-backed piece 3½″ × 14″, right sides facing. The raw edges should line up with the already attached bag piece and lining. Baste together. **E**

6 Pin the right side of the pocket lining piece 2″ × 14″ to the wrong side of the zipper. The zipper is now sandwiched between the pocket lining and the bag outside piece.

7 Use a zipper foot to stitch through all the layers. Press seams away from the zipper. **F**

8 Topstitch along both sides of the zipper.

MAKE THE OUTSIDE POCKET

1 Move the zipper pull down 1″ in from the bag edge. Cut the 2 ends of the zipper flush with the bag. Don't move your zipper pull at this point or you will lose it, because there is no stop for the zipper! **G**

2 Pin the right side of the pocket lining piece 9½″ × 14″ to the right sides of the 2″ × 14″ and 8″ × 14″ pocket lining pieces. Stitch together at the top and bottom, catching only the pocket lining pieces, not the bag, in your seam. **H**

3 Baste the pocket in place at the bag sides.

4 Stitch the 2 darts closed. (Refer to Sewing Darts, below.)

Sewing Darts

The V-shaped cutouts at the lower edge of the bag bottom are darts for adding shape to the bag. Close a dart by bringing the two sides of the V together, right sides facing. Make sure the raw edges of the bag bottom are matching. Pin together. Stitch the dart closed with a ¼″ seam, starting from the raw edge at the bottom to the fabric fold.

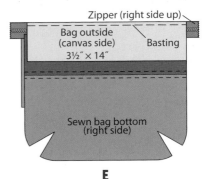

E

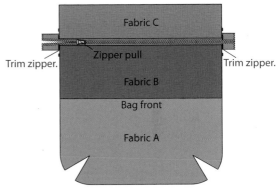

F Attach other half of zipper.

G Cut off extra zipper that extends beyond bag.

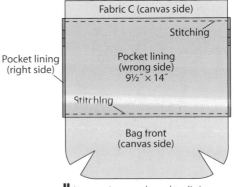

H Insert zippered pocket lining.

MAKE THE OUTSIDE BAG BACK

1 Using a ¼″ seam, sew the bag bottom piece (fabric A) to the bag outside piece 3½″ × 14″ (fabric C). Sew the bag piece 5½″ × 14″ (fabric B) to the other edge of the bag outside piece 3½″ × 14″. This piece is now referred to as the *bag back*. Note that the piecing sequence for the back is not the same as for the front.

2 Press all the seams open.

3 Using the bag back as a pattern, cut 1 piece from the canvas and 2 pieces from the bag lining fabric. I

4 Baste the canvas to the wrong side of the bag back along the top edge.

5 Topstitch on both sides of the 2 seams on the bag back.

6 Stitch the 2 darts at the bottom of the bag back. (Refer to Sewing Darts, page 31.)

7 Pin the bag back and the bag front pieces right sides together, matching darts. Stitch the bag together along the sides and bottom, leaving the top edge open. Note that the horizontal seams between fabrics B and C will not match—this is on purpose!

8 Press the seams open. Clip the seams and curves.

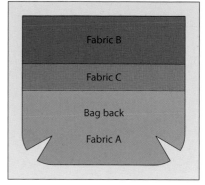

I Cut 1 piece of canvas and 2 pieces of lining fabric.

ASSEMBLE THE INSIDE ZIPPER

1 Mark the center of the 14″ zipper and the center of each of the 4 zipper placket pieces 2″ × 13″. **J**

2 Sandwich the zipper between 2 zipper placket pieces, with right sides of fabric facing each other. Match the marked centers on the zipper and the fabric.

3 Stitch the zipper in place, starting and stopping ½″ in from the ends of the fabric. Press the fabric away from the zipper. **K**

4 Repeat Steps 2 and 3 with the other side of the zipper and the 2 remaining zipper placket pieces.

5 Turn under the short raw ends of the fabric ¼″. Press and topstitch.

6 Topstitch along both sides of the zipper.

7 Trim this entire piece to 3″ wide, with the zipper in the center. **L**

8 Fold each of the fabric pieces 2″ × 2″ in half and press. Open up and fold under ¼″ on each raw end (all 4 sides). **M**

9 Refold the fabric pieces in half. Slip each of the tabs over an end of the zipper. Stitch in place by stitching around the entire perimeter of the zipper tab. This unit is now referred to as the *zipper placket*. **N**

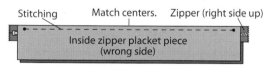

14″ zipper — Center

Inside zipper placket piece
2″ × 13″

J Mark centers.

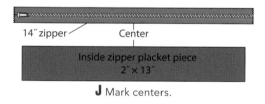

Stitching   Match centers.   Zipper (right side up)

Inside zipper placket piece
(wrong side)

K Sew zipper to inside zipper placket.

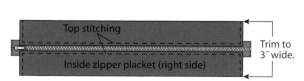

Top stitching

Inside zipper placket (right side)

Trim to 3″ wide.

L Topstitch zipper and trim zipper placket.

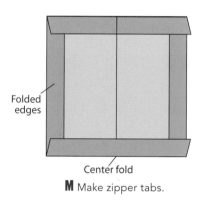

Folded edges

Center fold

M Make zipper tabs.

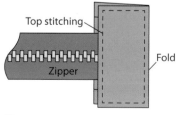

Top stitching

Zipper   Fold

N Attach zipper tab to zipper end.

MAKE THE BAG LINING

1 Cut 3″ off the top of both of the bag lining pieces that you cut out in Step 3 of Make the Outside Bag Back (page 32). Discard.

2 Pin the zipper placket to the cut bag lining, centering the zipper placket on the lining. The wrong side of the zipper placket will be facing the right side of the lining. Pin the right side of a lining piece 4″ × 14″ to the right side of the zipper placket. Stitch in place. **O**

3 Repeat Step 2 for the remaining lining piece.

4 Press the seams open.

5 Stitch the 2 darts at the bottom of each bag lining piece. (Refer to Sewing Darts, page 31.)

6 Sew the 2 bag lining pieces together, right sides facing, leaving the top open. Be careful not to catch the zipper in your seam.

7 Turn the bag lining right side out. You'll need to unzip the zipper to do this.

MAKE THE BAG STRAPS

1 Press the fusible interfacing to the wrong side of a strap piece 2½″ × 40″.

2 Stitch the interfaced bag strap to the other strap piece 2½″ × 40″ along a 40″ side. Use a ¼″ seam allowance and stop ½″ from an end. Press the seam open.

3 Turn under the raw edges of the long sides ¼″ and press. **P**

4 With the strap pieces right sides together, stitch an end closed, pivot at the corner, and stitch up 2″ onto the strap. Clip the corner, turn the strap right side out, and press.

5 With wrong sides together, pin the 2 folded edges of the bag strap flush. With the non-interfaced fabric facing down (next to the feed dogs on the machine), topstitch along the folded edge.

6 Topstitch close to the edge along the other side of the strap, pivot at the corner, and topstitch the closed end of the strap. **Q**

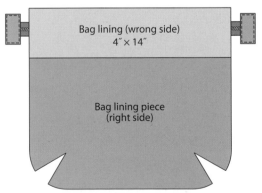

O Attach zipper placket to bag lining.

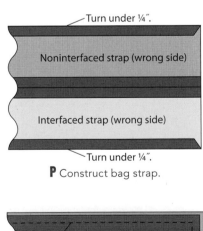

P Construct bag strap.

Q Topstitch bag straps.

7 Repeat Steps 1–6 with the strap pieces 2½″ × 18″. You do not need to close the ends of this strap piece.

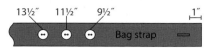

8 To make the strap adjustable, sew a buttonhole centered on the long strap. Place it 1″ in from the end of the bag strap.

9 Sew 3 buttons to the long bag strap. Place them 9½″, 11½″, and 13½″ in from the end of the bag strap. **R**

R Buttonhole and buttons for adjustable strap

FINISH THE BAG

1 Pin the long strap piece to the right side of the bag, matching the center of the short side of the strap with the bag side seam. Align the raw edges at the top of the bag. Stitch in place. Sew this seam twice to secure.

2 Slip the bag ring over the 18″ sewn strap piece and fold the 18″ strap in half. Pin to the other bag side seam, matching the raw edges. Stitch in place. **S**

3 Slip the lining (right side out) into the bag (wrong side out). Match the center seams and pin.

4 Stitch the bag lining and the bag outside pieces together at the top edge, leaving a 5″ opening.

5 Turn the bag right side out.

6 Turn under the raw edges of the opening and press in place. Press the top seam well.

7 Topstitch along the top edge of the bag, catching the opening as you sew.

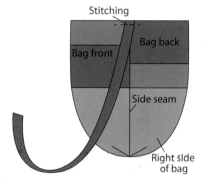

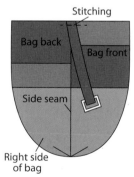

S Attach straps to bag.

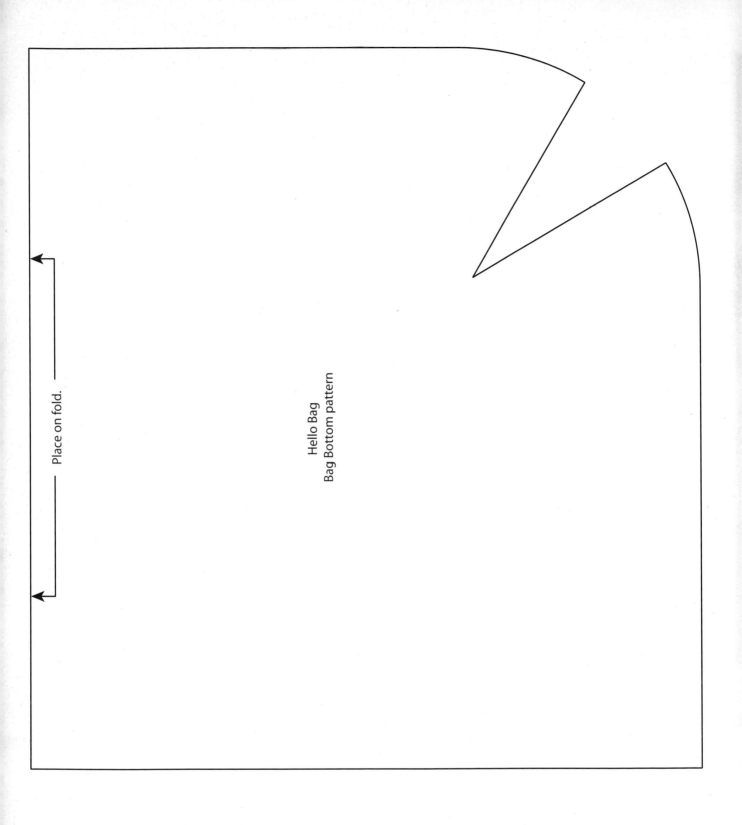

Place on fold.

Hello Bag
Bag Bottom pattern

Flag-o-Rama
Zip Pouches

FINISHED SIZES: *Union Jack pouch:* 8″ × 12″
Dutch flag pouch: 6½″ × 9″ • *Swiss flag pouch:* 5½″ × 7½″

Materials

Note: All of the duck cloth is distressed before cutting (see Distressing Duck Cloth and Canvas, page 14).

UNION JACK

- **White duck cloth:** ½ yard
- **Blue duck cloth:** ½ yard
- **Red duck cloth:** ½ yard
- **Fabric for lining and zipper tabs:** ¼ yard
- **Fusible fleece:** ½ yard
- **Paper-backed fusible web:** ¾ yard, 17″ wide
- **Zipper:** 12″ all-purpose
- **Thread:** red, white, and blue to match duck cloth
- **Recommended sewing machine needle:** top-stitch needle

DUTCH FLAG

- **White duck cloth:** ¼ yard
- **Red duck cloth:** ¼ yard
- **Blue duck cloth:** ⅛ yard
- **Fabric for lining and zipper tabs:** ½ yard
- **Fusible fleece:** ¼ yard
- **Paper-backed fusible web:** ¼ yard, 17″ wide
- **Zipper:** 9″ all-purpose
- **Thread:** white
- **Recommended sewing machine needle:** top-stitch needle

SWISS FLAG

- **Red duck cloth:** ¼ yard
- **White duck cloth:** scrap 5″ × 5″ square
- **Fabric for lining and zipper tabs:** 1 fat quarter (18″ × 22″), or ¼ yard
- **Fusible fleece:** ¼ yard
- **Paper-backed fusible web:** 1 piece 6″ × 6″ square
- **Zipper:** 9″ all-purpose
- **Thread:** red and white to match duck cloth
- **Recommended sewing machine needle:** top-stitch needle

My oldest daughter's dream is to grow up and travel the world. These fun little flag pouches will have to tide her over in the meantime—and hopefully hold foreign currency or travel documents in the future.

Cutting

UNION JACK

From blue duck cloth
- 2 pieces 9″ × 13″ for pouch front and back

From lining fabric
- 2 pieces 9″ × 13″ for lining
- 2 pieces 2″ × 2″ for zipper tabs

From fusible fleece
- 2 pieces 9″ × 13″

DUTCH FLAG

From white duck cloth
- 1 piece 7½″ × 10″ for pouch front

From red duck cloth
- 1 piece 7½″ × 10″ for pouch back
- 1 piece 2½″ × 10″ for stripe

From blue duck cloth
- 1 piece 2½″ × 10″ for stripe

From lining fabric
- 2 pieces 7½″ × 10″ for lining
- 2 pieces 2″ × 2″ for zipper tabs

From fusible fleece
- 2 pieces 7½″ × 10″

From paper-backed fusible web
- 2 pieces 2½″ × 10″

SWISS FLAG

From red duck cloth
- 2 pieces 6″ × 8½″ for pouch front and back

From lining fabric
- 2 pieces 6″ × 8½″ for lining
- 2 pieces 2″ × 2″ for zipper tabs

From fusible fleece
- 2 pieces 6″ × 8½″

Make the Union Jack Pouch

Refer to Union Jack patterns (pages 44 and 45).

All seam allowances are ½˝ unless otherwise noted.

MAKE THE APPLIQUÉS

White Duck Cloth

1 Trace the white Union Jack center piece pattern onto the paper side of the fusible web. Make sure to trace it on the fold of the paper-backed web.

2 Trace the pattern for the white corner pieces (2 of each pattern) onto the paper side of the fusible web. Leave about 3˝ of space between each shape to allow for rough cutting.

3 Roughly cut out the shapes, leaving about 1˝ all around.

4 With paper side up, press each pattern onto the white duck cloth.

5 Cut out the duck cloth, following your traced lines. You will have 5 pieces: 1 center, 2 upper right/lower left corner pieces, and 2 upper left/lower right corner pieces.

Red Duck Cloth

1 Trace the red Union Jack center piece pattern onto the paper side of the fusible web. Make sure to trace it on the fold of the paper-backed web.

2 Trace the pattern for the red corner pieces (4) onto the paper side of the fusible web

3 Roughly cut out the shapes, leaving about 1˝ all around.

4 With the paper side up, press each pattern onto the red duck cloth.

5 Cut out the duck cloth, following your traced lines. You will have 5 shapes: 1 center and 4 corner strips.

Union Jack pouch front

ASSEMBLE THE APPLIQUÉS

1 Remove the paper backing from the white corner pieces. With the fusible side down, place them diagonally in the 4 corners of the blue duck cloth 9″ × 13″. Place corner A in the upper right and lower left corners; place corner B in the upper left and lower right corners. Press to fuse in place. **A**

2 Remove the paper backing from the 4 red corner strips. Place them on top of the white corner pieces, fusible side down. Note that the red corner pieces are not centered on the white corner pieces. Trim the corners to match the blue rectangle. Press to fuse in place. **B**

3 Using a top-stitch needle with matching red and white thread, top-stitch the edge of each of the red and white corner pieces.

4 Remove the paper backing from the white Union Jack center piece and place this piece on top of the corner pieces. It should fit perfectly in the center, with raw edges matching the blue rectangle. Press to fuse in place. **C**

TIP *Before you stitch or press any pieces in place, make sure they all fit together properly.*

5 Remove the paper backing from the red Union Jack center piece and place it on top of the white Union Jack piece. Press to fuse in place. **D**

6 Using a top-stitch needle with matching red and white thread, top-stitch around the edges of each center cross.

ASSEMBLE THE UNION JACK POUCH

1 Apply fusible fleece to the wrong side of the 2 lining pieces 9″ × 13″.

2 Trim the zipper to 12″, cutting off the zipper stop at each end.

3 Make 2 zipper tabs and attach to the ends of the zipper, following the instructions for Make Zipper Tabs (page 16).

4 To complete the pouch, follow the instructions for Constructing a Basic Zip Pouch (page 16).

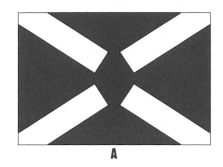
A

Trim to match corners.
B

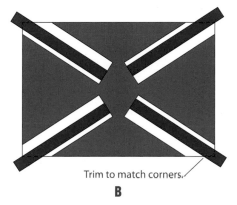
C

D

Make the Dutch Flag Pouch

All seam allowances are ½″ unless otherwise noted.

ASSEMBLE THE APPLIQUÉS

1 With paper side up, press fusible web 2½″ × 10″ onto the wrong side of the red and blue duck cloth pieces 2½″ × 10″.

2 Remove the paper backing from both strips.

3 Place the red strip along the top edge of the white duck cloth piece 7½″ × 10″, right sides facing up. Press to fuse in place.

4 Place the blue strip along the bottom edge of the white duck cloth piece 7½″ × 10″. Press to fuse in place.

5 Using a top-stitch needle and white thread, topstitch close to the edge of both pieces.

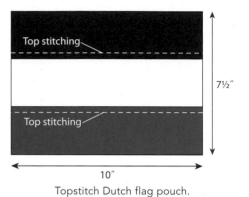

Topstitch Dutch flag pouch.

ASSEMBLE THE DUTCH FLAG POUCH

1 Apply fusible fleece to the wrong side of the 2 lining pieces 7½″ × 10″.

2 Trim the zipper to 9″, cutting off the zipper stop at each end.

3 Make 2 zipper tabs and attach to the ends of the zipper, following the instructions for Make Zipper Tabs (page 16).

4 To complete the Dutch Flag pouch, follow the instructions for Constructing a Basic Zip Pouch (page 16).

Dutch flag pouch front

Make the Swiss Flag Pouch

Refer to Swiss Flag pattern (below).

All seam allowances are ½˝ unless otherwise noted.

ASSEMBLE THE APPLIQUÉ

1 Trace the Swiss Flag pattern onto a piece of paper-backed fusible web. Roughly cut it out.

2 Press web onto the wrong side of the white duck cloth scrap 5˝ × 5˝. Cut out the duck cloth by following the traced lines of the pattern.

3 Peel off the paper backing and center the shape on the piece of red duck cloth 6˝ × 8½˝. Press to fuse in place.

4 Using a top-stitch needle and white thread, topstitch around the white appliqué piece.

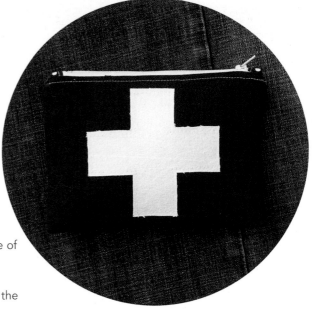

Swiss flag pouch front

ASSEMBLE THE SWISS FLAG POUCH

1 Apply fusible fleece to the wrong side of the 2 lining pieces.

2 Trim zipper to 7½˝, cutting off the zipper stop at each end.

3 Make 2 zipper tabs and attach to the ends of the zipper, following the instructions for Make Zipper Tabs (page 16).

4 To complete the Swiss flag pouch, follow the instructions for Constructing a Basic Zip Pouch (page 16).

Flag-o-Rama Zip Pouches
Swiss Flag pattern
Cut 1.
White

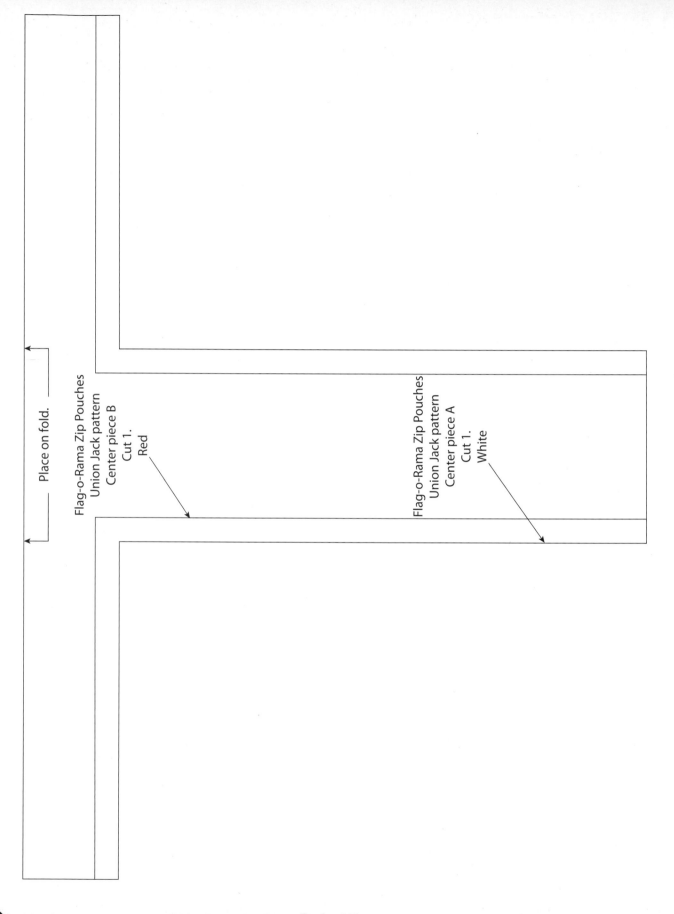

Place on fold.

Flag-o-Rama Zip Pouches
Union Jack pattern
Center piece B
Cut 1.
Red

Flag-o-Rama Zip Pouches
Union Jack pattern
Center piece A
Cut 1.
White

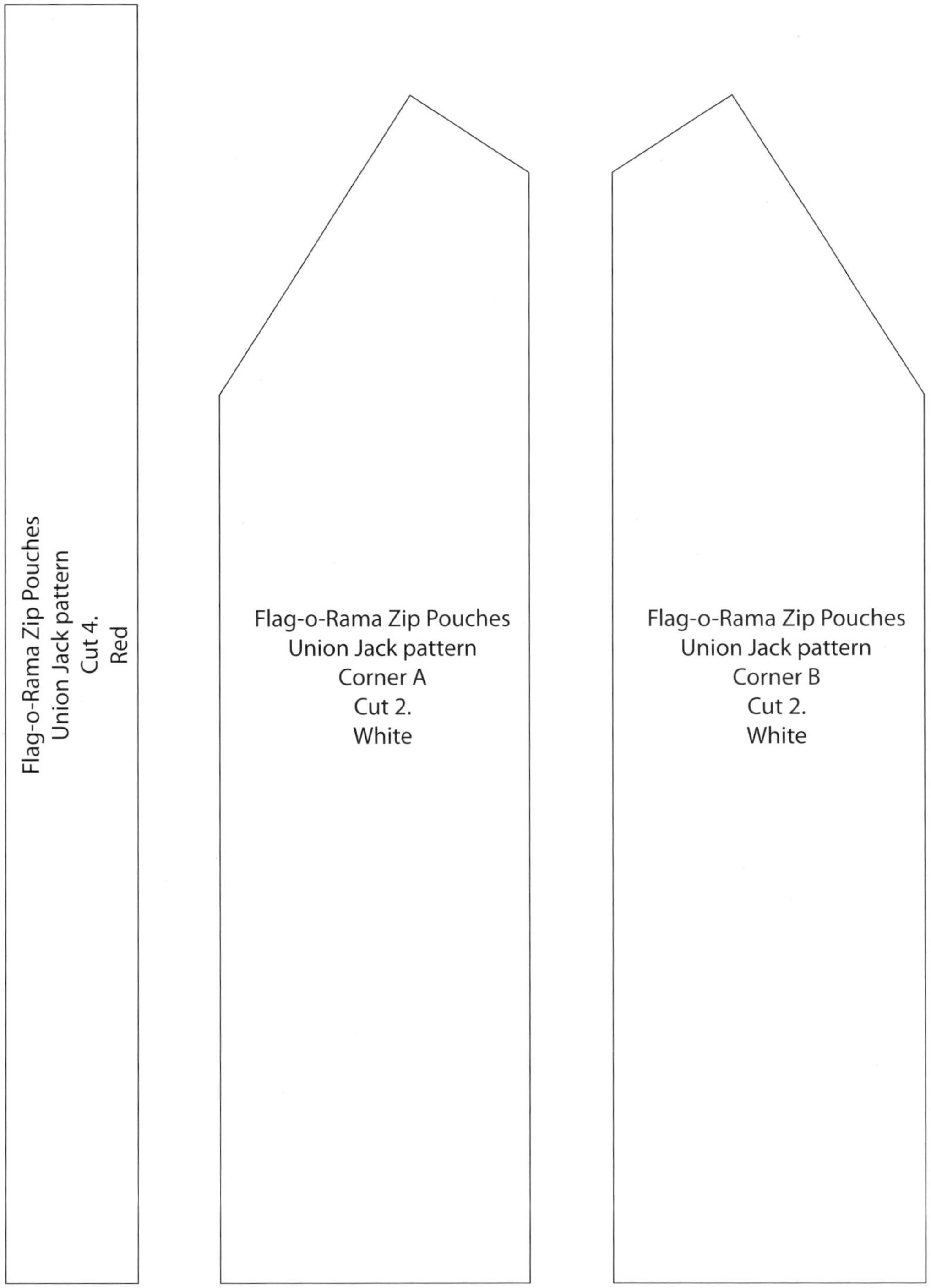

Flag-o-Rama Zip Pouches
Union Jack pattern
Cut 4.
Red

Flag-o-Rama Zip Pouches
Union Jack pattern
Corner A
Cut 2.
White

Flag-o-Rama Zip Pouches
Union Jack pattern
Corner B
Cut 2.
White

I Left My Heart in Pouch

FINISHED SIZE: 6″ × 14″

When my oldest daughter headed off to another state for college, we collected things to remind her of home. I love maps and thought it might be fun to figure out how to sew with one. A stitched heart encircles her hometown.

Materials

- **Paper map:** at least 15″ × 31″
- **Canvas:** ½ yard
- **Fabric for lining:** 1 fat quarter (18″ × 22″)
- **Iron-on vinyl:** ¾ yard
- **Zipper:** 14″ all-purpose (check size of zipper)
- **Embroidery floss:** red
- **Recommended sewing machine feet:** nonstick foot, zipper foot

Cutting

From map

- 2 pieces 7″ × 15″
  Place the city you want to encircle just off the center of one of the pieces.

From iron-on vinyl

- 2 pieces 7″ × 15″

From canvas

- 2 pieces 7″ × 15″

From fat quarter

- 2 pieces 7″ × 15″

Make the I Left My Heart in _____ Pouch

All sewing is done with a nonstick foot. All seam allowances are ½" unless otherwise noted.

ASSEMBLE THE OUTSIDE

1 Press the paper map pieces with an iron on low setting to smooth out folds and wrinkles.

2 With paper backing side up, iron the vinyl onto the right sides of the 2 map pieces. Follow the vinyl manufacturer's instructions for ironing. Set aside the paper backing pieces.

Backstitch with embroidery floss.

3 Draw a heart on a map piece in the location you want, using a very light pen or pencil.

4 Hand stitch around the heart using 6 strands of embroidery floss and a backstitch pattern.

5 Pin the canvas pieces to the wrong sides of the pouch outer pieces. Baste the bottom edges.

Embroidered heart on front of pouch

ASSEMBLE THE I LEFT MY HEART IN _____ POUCH

To complete the pouch, follow Constructing a Basic Zip Pouch (page 16). Note that this pouch does not have zipper tabs.

TIP *If your pouch is in need of pressing after you turn it right side out, you can use the paper backing that you peeled off the fusible vinyl as a "pressing cloth." Place the shiny side of the backing against the vinyl and press on a low setting. Do not put the iron directly on the vinyl-coated fabric because it will melt!*

Upcycled Jacket
Tablet Clutch

FINISHED SIZE: 8″ × 10″

> **My husband** was about to throw away an old wool jacket. Rather than see nice fabric go to waste, I decided to make an iPad case from it. Then I realized it could be pretty too. In fact, this one is so stylish, it can double as a clutch for a fancy evening out!

Materials

- **Fabric for clutch exterior:** men's wool jacket (The larger, the better!)
- **Fabric for lining:** ½ yard
- **Timtex:** ½ yard
- **Ribbon for embellishment:** 1 yard, ½″ wide
- **Fusible tape:** 1 yard, ½″ wide
- **Sew-on snap:** 1, size 10
- **Recommended sewing machine foot:** walking foot

Cutting

Refer to Clutch Flap patterns (page 53).

TIP *The back of the jacket provides the most fabric for cutting out your pieces. Pick the largest, flattest, and straightest portions of the back of the jacket. Try to avoid darts or other shaped areas.*

From men's jacket

- 2 pieces 8½″ × 11″ for clutch front and back (If there is a jacket seam in the cut pieces, place it vertically and off center.)
- 1 piece for clutch flap from Clutch Flap pattern 1

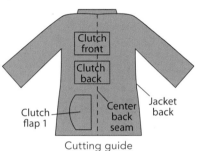

Cutting guide

From lining fabric

- 2 pieces 8½″ × 11″ for clutch lining
- 1 piece for flap lining from Clutch Flap pattern 1

From Timtex

- 2 pieces 7½″ × 10″
- 1 piece from Clutch Flap pattern 2

TIP *You can resize this clutch for another gadget. Using a tape measure, measure around the entire gadget in the lengthwise direction. Divide the measurement by 2, and add 1″ for seam allowances and another 1″ for ease. This is the length of the rectangle for the front and back pieces.*

● *Measure around the entire device on the short side. Divide the measurement by 2, and add 1″ for seam allowances and 1″ for ease. This is the width of the rectangle. Adjust the sizes of the flap patterns to match the new rectangle size.*

Make the Tablet Clutch

All seam allowances are ½" unless otherwise noted.

This clutch is a very snug fit for the iPad 2. Use a lightweight cotton for the lining and be careful that your seam allowances are no larger than ½" or your tablet computer might not fit.

MAKE THE CLUTCH OUTSIDE

1 Cut 2 lengths of ribbon 8½" each and 2 lengths of fusible tape 8½" each. Cover the jacket seams on the clutch front and back pieces with ribbon, using fusible tape to attach. Press to fuse in place.

TIP *Use a pressing cloth between the fused ribbon and iron to avoid getting bits of fusible tape stuck on your iron.*

2 Center the Timtex pieces 7½" × 10" on the wrong side of the clutch front and back pieces 8½" × 11". Baste together on the 10" sides only. **A**

3 Pin together the clutch front and back pieces with right sides facing. Stitch together on 3 sides, leaving the top (11" side) open.

4 Clip the corners, press the seams open, and turn the clutch right side out.

5 Press under the top raw edge of the clutch ½".

MAKE THE CLUTCH LINING

1 Pin together the 2 lining pieces 8½" × 11" with right sides facing.

2 Stitch the lining on 3 sides, leaving the top seam (11" side) open.

3 Clip the corners, and trim the seam allowances to ¼". Press the seams open.

4 Press under the top raw edge of lining ½".

ASSEMBLE THE CLUTCH

1 Slip the clutch lining (wrong side out) into the clutch outside (right side out). Match the side seams and the top folded edges. Check the fit and adjust the seam allowances as needed.

2 Pin together the lining and the outside at the top of the clutch. Topstitch close to the edge around the top. **B**

TIP *When sewing many layers of fabric together, use a walking foot on your machine for a better result.*

3 Press well.

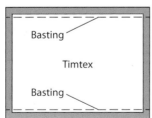

A Baste Timtex to clutch front and back pieces.

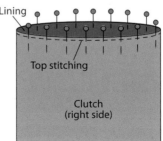

B Topstitch near top edge of clutch.

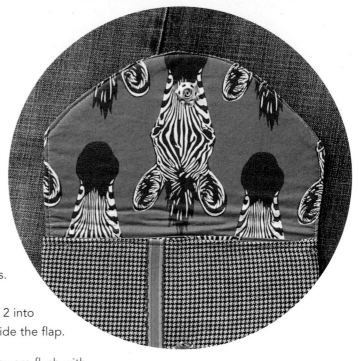

ASSEMBLE THE FLAP

1 Pin together the flap outside and the flap lining, with right sides facing.

2 Sew around the curved edge, leaving open the top of the flap.

3 Clip the curves and turn the flap right side out. Press.

4 Insert the Timtex piece cut from Clutch Flap pattern 2 into the flap. Trim the Timtex as needed so that it fits inside the flap.

5 Press under the raw edges of the flap top so that they are flush with the top of the Timtex. If you don't have enough fabric to press under, trim the Timtex ¼" along the straight (top) edge. Baste along the folded edge.

6 Pin the basted edge of the lining side of the flap to the right side of the clutch back. The edge of the flap should be 1" below the top edge of the clutch.

7 Topstitch the flap in place along the folded edge. Be careful to keep the clutch front free. **C**

FINISH THE CLUTCH

1 Place the iPad inside the case. Fold over the flap and mark the location for the snap on both the inside of the flap and the outside of the case front.

2 Hand sew the snap in place.

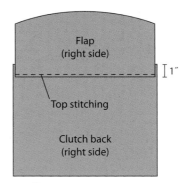

C Stitch flap to clutch.

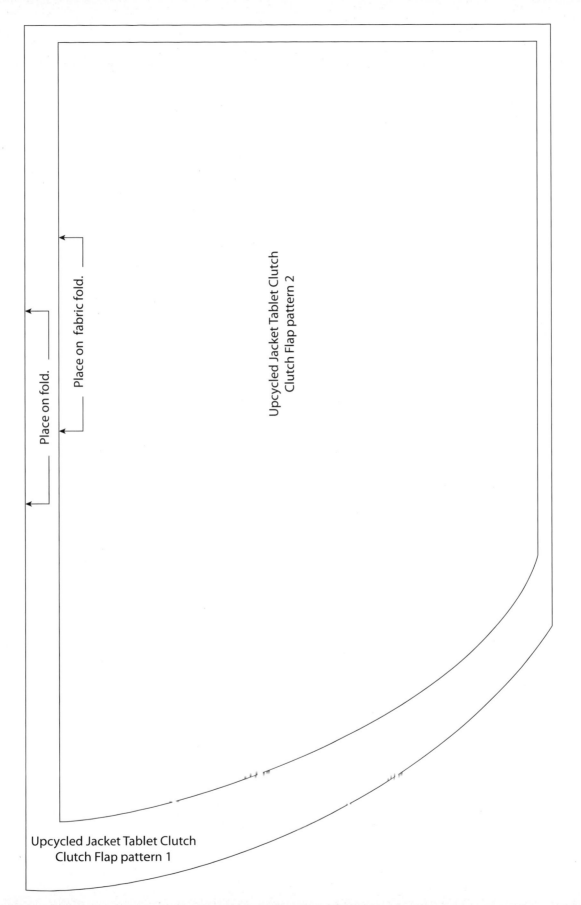

Place on fold.

Place on fabric fold.

Upcycled Jacket Tablet Clutch
Clutch Flap pattern 2

Upcycled Jacket Tablet Clutch
Clutch Flap pattern 1

Goodbye Travel Blanket

FINISHED SIZE: 55˝ × 70˝

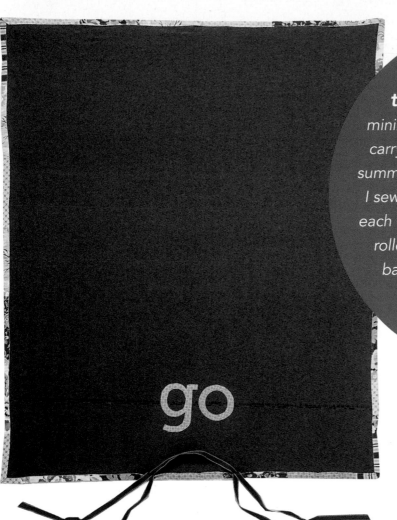

My family loves to travel. To keep baggage to a minimum, we have a rule: "If you can't carry it yourself, don't bring it!" A few summers ago, for a big international trip, I sewed a ribbon to a travel blanket for each of my kids so that it could be easily rolled up and attached to a carry-on bag. The idea worked so well that I decided to make one from scratch, but even cuter.

TIP *The handle on this blanket is designed to slip over the handle of a rolling carry-on bag.*

Materials

- **Polar fleece:** 2 yards, 60″ wide

- **Fabric for binding:** 14 jelly roll strips (2½″ × 42″ each)

- **Fabric for appliqué:** 2 pieces about 9″ × 11″ each

- **Paper-backed fusible web:** 2 pieces about 9″ × 11″ each

- **Cotton grosgrain ribbon:** 3¼ yards, 1″ wide

- **Recommended sewing machine foot:** walking foot

- **Tools:** Fabric-safe marking pen

Cutting

From polar fleece
- 1 piece 55″ × 70″

From jelly roll
- 28 strips 2½″ × 10″
- 7 strips 2½″ × 40″

From ribbon
- 1 piece 15″ long
- 2 pieces 48″ long

Make the Goodbye Travel Blanket

All seam allowances are ¼″ unless otherwise noted.

MAKE THE PATCHWORK BINDING

1 Sew together the 28 strips 2½″ × 10″ along the short sides. Try not to have 2 of the same prints next to each other. You will end up with a *very* long strip of fabric. Press seams to 1 side. This piece is now called *binding strip A*.

2 Sew together the 7 strips 2½″ × 40″ along the short sides. Press seams to 1 side. This piece is now called *binding strip B*.

3 Sew binding strip A to binding strip B lengthwise, right sides together. Press the seam open.

4 Trim binding strip B to match binding strip A. **A**

5 Fold binding strip lengthwise along the seam, wrong sides together, so that the raw edges are even. Press along the fold. This piece is now referred to as *the binding*.

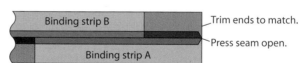

A Sew binding strips together along a long edge.

BIND THE BLANKET

1 Lay the fleece out flat, wrong side facing up. Align the raw edge of the binding to the raw edge of the fleece. The right side of the binding that was made up of 10″ strips (binding strip A) should be facing the back side of the fleece.

2 Sew the binding to the fleece, using a walking foot and a ⅜″ seam allowance. Leave 6″ of the binding unstitched when you begin sewing, and do not start at a corner. **B**

3 To turn the corners, follow the instructions for Attach the Binding (page 18).

4 Continue stitching until you are 4″ away from where you started. Measure the binding strips so that they will match up perfectly with the blanket. Mark this point on both binding ends with a fabric-safe marking pen.

5 Unfold the binding and stitch the binding ends together at the marking, right sides facing each other. Trim the seam allowance to ¼″.

6 Refold the binding and finish stitching the binding to the blanket.

7 Press the binding and the seam allowance away from the blanket.

8 Bring the binding to the front of the blanket so that the folded edge just covers the stitching line. Press and pin in place. Do not stitch yet.

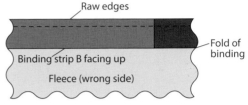

Raw edges

Fold of binding

Binding strip B facing up

Fleece (wrong side)

B Sew binding to wrong side of blanket.

TIPS When pressing fleece, make sure your iron is set for synthetics, and use a pressing cloth to avoid damaging the fleece.

● For holding binding in place before stitching, I prefer to use specially designed binding clips (such as Clover binding clips) rather than straight pins.

ATTACH THE RIBBON

1 Choose 1 of the 55″ blanket sides to be the bottom. Measure in 22″ from each side and mark those points with pins.

2 Pin the 2 ends of the 15″ ribbon strip under the binding at the marked positions.

3 Fold the 48″ ribbons in half crosswise. Pin the folded edges next to the ends of the ribbon loop, hiding the raw edges under the binding.

4 Trim the raw edges of the ribbons with a diagonal cut to prevent fraying. **C**

5 Sew the binding down on the front of the blanket, stitching close to the folded edge. Catch the ribbons under the binding as you sew. Reinforce the binding where the ribbons are attached by adding another row of stitching on top of the first.

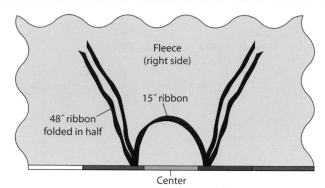

C Place ends of ribbon under binding.

ASSEMBLE THE APPLIQUÉ

1 Make the "go" appliqué following the instructions for Using Computer Fonts as Appliqué Patterns (page 10). I used the Museo Slab font printed at 785 picas, which is 8″ tall.

2 Place the appliqué 6″ up from the bottom edge and centered between the ribbons. Fuse the appliqué to the blanket (remember to use a pressing cloth between the iron and the appliqué).

3 Finish the edge of the appliqué with a straight stitch, following the instructions for Appliqué Stitching (page 12). **D**

D Sew appliqué to blanket using straight stitch.

TIP *To roll up the blanket, fold it into thirds widthwise and then fold it in half lengthwise. Roll the blanket up starting at the side that does not have ribbons attached. Tie the ribbons around the blanket to secure the roll.*

Do Not Lose This Folder

FINISHED SIZE: 9˝ × 11½˝ folded (large enough for a letter-sized folder)

Materials

- **Laminated cotton:** ¾ yard
- **Fabric for appliqué:** 1 fat quarter (18″ × 22″), or scrap about 8″ × 11″
- **Manila folder:** standard 8½″ × 11″
- **Nonslip elastic headbands:** 2
- **Paper-backed fusible web:** 1 piece 8″ × 11″
- **Ribbon:** 1 yard, ⅜″ wide
- **Recommended sewing machine presser foot:** nonstick foot
- **Tools:** pressing cloth

TIP *You can find nonslip elastic head-bands in the hair accessory section in drug stores, grocery stores, or general retailers.*

For reasons I will never understand, my kids can spend hours doing their homework (or other projects) only to haphazardly throw the completed work into their backpacks or leave it behind. It's no big surprise that they lose a lot of their things. This sturdy and bright folder is designed to hold those important papers.

Cutting

From laminated cotton

- 1 piece 12¾″ × 19″ for folder outside
- 2 pieces 9½″ × 12¾″ for folder inside

Make the Folder

All sewing is done with a nonstick sewing foot. All seam allowances are ½˝ unless otherwise noted.

ASSEMBLE THE APPLIQUÉ

1 Make the "do not lose" appliqué following the instructions for Using Computer Fonts as Appliqué Patterns (page 10). I used Chunk Five Ex font in 220 point, or about 2⅜˝ tall.

2 Peel off the paper backing from the letters and place them on the folder outside piece, web side down. With the outside piece folded in half, the bottom of the letters should sit 1¾˝ above the fold. **A**

3 Fuse the letters into place using a pressing cloth. *Do not place the iron directly on the laminated cotton!* The letters will stick to the laminated cotton but not very securely. Don't move the folder around too much after you press them or they might fall off.

4 Finish the edges of the letters with a straight stitch following the instructions for Appliqué Stitching (page 12).

A Place letters on folder.

ASSEMBLE THE FOLDER

1 Turn under ½" on a long side of the folder piece 9½" × 12¾".
Finger-press and stitch. Repeat for the other folder piece 9½" × 12¾".

2 Cut each of the 2 elastic headbands to 12¾" long.

3 Center an elastic strip on the right side of each folder inside piece,
raw edges matching. **B**

4 Stitch the elastic close to the edge of the fabric. Add another
stitching line ⅞" in from each edge.

5 Cut 2 pieces of ribbon 18" long.

6 Pin a piece of ribbon to the center of each folder outside edge 12¾".

7 With right sides facing, pin a folder inside piece to each end of the
folder outside piece. Match the raw edges, and stitch in place. Clip
the corners of the seam allowance. **C**

8 Turn the folder right side out.

9 Trim off the tab of the manila folder. Slip the folder into the laminated
fabric folder.

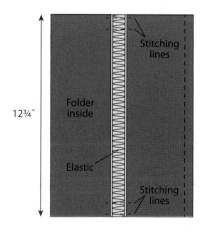

B Center elastic on folder inside.

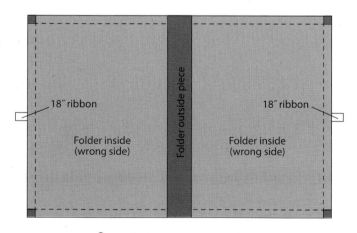

C Sew folder pieces along edges.

JUST FOR GUYS

There are few things that **strike fear** into the heart of a sewist more than the idea of making something for a teenage boy! When writing this book, I challenged myself to come up with projects designed specifically with teenage boys in mind. Using my son and his friends as experts, I soaked up all of their ideas for things they would want and came up with these projects.

T-Shirt Pillows

FINISHED SIZES: *Strip pillow:* 16″ × 16″ • *Square pillow:* 18″ × 18″

Strip Pillow

Materials

- **T-shirt:** can be any size, but must be at least 9″ × 16″, including the graphic
- **Cotton fabric:** 2 fat quarters (18″ × 22″ each)
- **Piping:** 2½-yard package of premade piping
- **Shape-Flex woven fusible interfacing:** 1 package 20″ × 45″, or 1¼ yards 19″–20″ wide
- **Pillow form:** 16″ × 16″ square

Cutting

Change the size of the fabric strips depending on the size of the graphic cut from your T-shirt. The measurements provided here worked with my shirt, but you may need to change them to work with yours. Once pieced, the pillow front should measure 16″ × 16″.

From T-shirt front
- 1 piece 9″ × 16″ (include graphic element)

From T-shirt back
- 1 piece 16″ × 16″

From fat quarters
- 1 strip 2½″ × 16″
- 1 strip 5½″ × 16″

From fusible interfacing
- 1 strip 9″ × 16″
- 1 piece 16″ × 16″

I love T-shirts. I admit to picking up more than a few as souvenirs when we travel. Because of this, quite a few of our T-shirts have sentimental meaning to my family. My first thought was to make a quilt with them, but then I decided that a pillow might be a little bit more fun.

Make the Strip Pillow

All seams are ¼″ unless otherwise noted.

1 Iron the Shape-Flex to the wrong side of the T-shirt pieces 9″ × 16″ and 16″ × 16″, following the manufacturer's instructions. This will stabilize the stretchy T-shirt knit.

2 Sew the fabric strip 2½″ × 16″ to the top of the T-shirt front 9″ × 16″. Sew the fabric strip 5½″ × 16″ to the bottom of the T-shirt front. Press seams open.

3 Topstitch along both sides of the 2 seams, using a matching or contrasting color thread.

4 Attach the piping to the front of the pillow following the instructions for Working with Piping (page 14).

5 Pin together the pillow front and the pillow back pieces, right sides facing. Stitch around the edge, with the front on top, along the same stitching line you used to attach the piping. Leave an 8″ opening in the bottom of the pillow to turn it right side out.

6 Clip the corners and turn the pillow right side out.

7 Insert the pillow form into the pillow and slipstitch the opening closed.

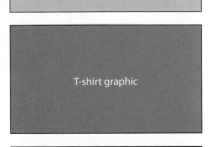

T-shirt graphic

Pillow front layout

Square Pillow

Materials

- **T-shirt:** large enough so that graphic fits in a 13″ × 13″ square
- **Cotton fabric:** 1 fat quarter (18″ × 22″)
- **Shape-Flex woven fusible interfacing:** 1 package 20″ × 45″, or 1¼ yards 19″–20″ wide
- **Pillow form:** 18″ × 18″ square

Cutting

From the T-shirt front
- 1 piece 13″ × 13″

From the T-shirt back
- 1 piece 18″ × 18″

From the fat quarter
- 2 strips 3″ × 13″
- 2 strips 3″ × 18″

From the fusible interfacing
- 1 piece 13″ × 13″
- 1 piece 18″ × 18″

TIP *Does your T-shirt have an image on the back? If so, make sure that you include it on the back of your pillow!*

Make the Square Pillow

1 Iron Shape-Flex onto the wrong side of the 2 T-shirt pieces, 13″ × 13″ and 18″ × 18″, following manufacturer's instructions. This will stabilize the T-shirt knit.

2 Sew the 2 strips 3″ × 13″ to the top and the bottom of the T-shirt front 13″ × 13″. Press the seams to 1 side. Topstitch.

3 Sew the 2 strips 3″ × 18″ to the sides of the T-shirt front. Press the seams to 1 side. Topstitch.

4 Finish the pillow by following Steps 4–7 of the instructions for Make the Strip Pillow (page 66).

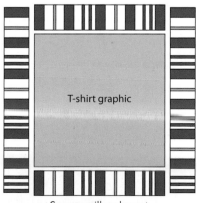

Square pillow layout

Sports Team Tablet Case

FINISHED SIZE: 9¾″ × 11″

We are big fans of college sports in our house. One day, rather than give away one of my son's favorite University of Louisville sweatshirts, I decided to reuse the patches on the sweatshirt in a sewing project. I liked the look and began searching thrift and antique stores for vintage patches to use on projects. It's hard to find things that boys will like as embellishments on sewing projects, but these patches are perfect. The graphics are great, and they will give any project you make a fun and unique feel.

TIP *This tablet computer case features a back zip pocket to store extra items, like headphones and papers, and it's padded with foam for an extra layer of protection.*

Materials

- **Canvas for outside of case:** 1 yard
- **Fabric for lining:** ½ yard fine-wale corduroy, flannel, or other soft fabric
- **Foam (may be called auto liner foam):** ½ yard, ¼″ thick
- **fast2fuse (lightweight):** ½ yard
- **Zipper:** 12″ all-purpose
- **Sew-on snap:** 30mm size (¹³⁄₁₆″)
- **Patch for embellishment**
- **Top-stitching thread**
- **Recommended sewing machine feet and needle:** walking foot, zipper foot, top-stitch needle

TIP *Look for patches you can recycle from sweatshirts, baseball caps, and jackets. You could also use vintage Boy Scout patches.*

Cutting

Before cutting, distress the canvas following the instructions for Distressing Duck Cloth and Canvas (page 14).

From distressed canvas
- 1 piece 10″ × 12″ for front
- 1 piece 10″ × 12″ for zippered pocket lining
- 1 piece 10″ × 12″ for flap front
- 1 piece 10″ × 12″ for flap lining
- 1 piece 4″ × 10″ for zipper panel
- 1 piece 10″ × 10″ for zipper panel

From fast2fuse
- 1 piece 10″ × 12″

From lining
- 2 pieces 10″ × 12″

From ¼″ foam
- 2 pieces 10″ × 12″

Make the Sports Team Tablet Case

All seams are ½″ unless otherwise noted.

MAKE THE CASE OUTSIDE

1 Place the zipper along the upper edge of the zipper panel piece 4″ × 10″. Pin the zipper along the 10″ edge, with the top stop of the zipper aligned with the short side of the fabric piece. The right side of the zipper should face the right side of the fabric. Use a zipper foot to stitch together. Zigzag stitch over the fabric's raw edge. **A**

2 Pin the other half of the zipper to the large zipper panel piece 10″ × 10″. The right side of the zipper should face the right side of the fabric. Use a zipper foot to stitch together. Be careful not to catch the small panel. Zigzag stitch over the fabric's raw edge. **B**

3 Press the seams away from the zipper. Topstitch near the edge of the zipper. Trim off excess zipper above the bottom zipper stop.

4 Trim the entire piece to 10″ × 12″. (Don't worry if you need to cut off a lot of fabric—extra was added to the measurements to give you flexibility when inserting your zipper.) **C**

5 Pin the wrong side of the sewn zipper piece on top of the right side of the pocket lining piece 10″ × 12″. Baste around all of the edges. This is the case back.

6 Stitch the case front piece 10″ × 12″ to the case back, right sides facing. Stitch around 3 sides, leaving open the 12″ side where the zipper ends. Clip the corners. Set aside.

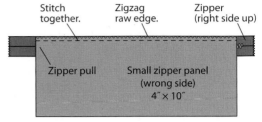

A Stitch zipper to small zipper panel.

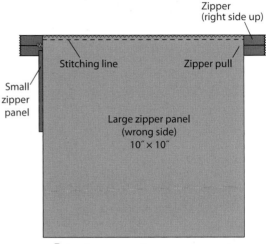

B Stitch zipper to large zipper panel.

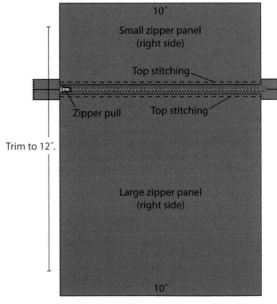

C

MAKE THE OUTSIDE FLAP

1 Iron the fast2fuse interfacing onto the wrong side of the flap 10″ × 12″.

2 Stitch the patch to the bottom right side of flap outside piece, 1½″ in from the corner. **D**

3 Pin the flap front and the flap lining together, right sides facing. Stitch along 3 sides, leaving the 12″ side that is farthest from the patch open. **E**

4 Trim seam allowances at the corners. Turn the flap right side out and press well.

5 Topstitch along the outer edge of the flap piece, using contrasting thread if you like.

D Sew patch to flap front.

MAKE THE CASE LINING

1 Place the 2 lining pieces right sides together.

2 Place a piece of foam on top of the wrong side of each piece of corduroy. You should have a sandwich of foam "bread" with a "filling" of lining. **F**

3 Stitch around 3 sides as you did for the case outside (leaving a 12″ side open). Go slowly and use a walking foot. Trim the seam allowances to ¼″. Turn right side out.

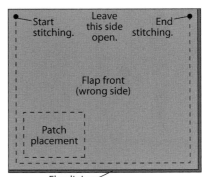

E Sew flap and flap lining together on 3 sides.

F Sandwich 2 pieces of corduroy with foam pieces.

FINISH THE SPORTS TEAM TABLET CASE

1 Slip the flap into the case with the right side of the flap front facing the right side of the case back. Match and pin the raw edge of the case back (the part with the zipper) flush with the raw edge of the flap. Baste in place. **F**

2 Slip the padded lining piece into the case, right sides together. Pin the padded lining to the front and back of the case.

3 Stitch around the raw edge of the case, starting about 2″ from the center front, around to the back, then back around to the front, leaving a 4″ opening to turn the case right side out. Trim the foam seam allowances to ⅛″. **G**

4 Turn right side out. Press well.

5 Turn under the raw edge of the opening in the case so that it is in line with the rest of the case. Pin in place.

6 Topstitch along the front edge of the case, catching the opening as you sew. Use a walking foot to keep the layers together. **H**

7 Hand sew a large snap to the case.

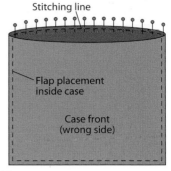

F Baste flap to back cover of case.

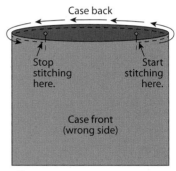

G Stitch around edge of case, leaving 4″ opening.

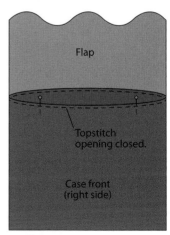

H Topstitch around case.

Small Tech Case

FINISHED SIZE: 3¾″ × 5½″

My son is always carrying around an electronic gadget of some sort. I am also always finding headphones all over the house. I designed this case for him to keep both things in the same place. This one's made to fit an iPhone 5 but could easily be resized to fit any type of gadget. Elastic headbands are used in the construction of this case.

Materials

- **Gray duck cloth:** ½ yard
- **Red duck cloth:** scrap at least 4″ × 6″
- **Plastic canvas sheet:** piece at least 7″ × 11″
- **Nonslip elastic headbands:** 2
- **Paper-backed fusible web:** scrap at least 4″ × 13″

Distress the canvas by following the instructions for Distressing Duck Cloth and Canvas (page 14).

TIP *You can find nonslip elastic headbands in the hair accessory section in drug stores, grocery stores, or general retailers.*

Cutting

From gray duck cloth
- 1 piece 6″ × 8″ for case outside
- 1 piece 6″ × 8″ for case inside
- 1 piece 4″ × 4″ for case pocket

From red duck cloth
- 2 pieces 1½″ × 6″ for case spines

From fusible web
- 2 pieces 1½″ × 6″

From plastic canvas
- 2 pieces 3″ × 5″

Make the Small Tech Case

All seam allowances are ¼″ unless otherwise noted.

MAKE THE CASE OUTSIDE

1 On the right side of a gray piece 6″ × 8″ mark the midpoint on each long side. Use a fabric-safe pen to draw a line connecting the marked points. This is the center front.

2 Apply fusible web to the wrong side of a red piece 1½″ × 6″. Mark the midpoint on each short side. Use a fabric-safe pen to draw a line connecting the marked points. This is the center front of the spine piece.

3 Remove the paper backing from the red fabric piece.

4 With the web side down, position the red fabric piece on the right side of the gray fabric piece, matching the center fronts. Press to fuse in place.

5 Topstitch the long edges of the red spine piece.

6 Cut a piece of elastic headband 6″ long.

Note
If desired, apply decorative appliqué to the bottom right corner of the case outside.

7 Pin the band to the case outside piece, parallel to the center front and 1″ in from the right edge. Stitch down the ends of the elastic, close to the edge of the case. **A**

MAKE THE CASE INSIDE

Attach the Elastic

1 Cut 3 pieces of elastic headband each 4″ long.

2 Cut 1 piece of elastic headband 3″ long.

3 On the right side of the gray inside piece 6″ × 8″, mark the center front with a fabric-safe marking pen.

4 Pin the 3 pieces of 4″ elastic headband horizontally on the right half of the case inside piece: Pin a piece 1″ down from the top and pin another piece 1″ up from the bottom. Center the third elastic piece between the first 2.

5 Stitch the elastic in place at the ends, close to the case edge and the case center. **B**

6 Pin the 3″ piece of elastic vertically on the case, 1″ in from the left edge of the case. Stitch the ends of the elastic to the case. Sew another row of stitching at the midpoint of the elastic. **B**

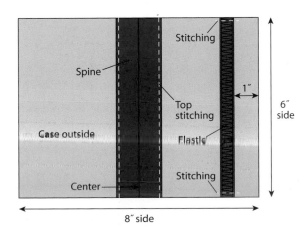

A Assemble outside of case.

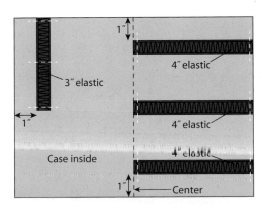

B Assemble inside of case.

Attach the Pocket and Inside Spine

1 Fold under ¼″ along a side of the gray pocket piece 4″ × 4″. Press and topstitch along the fold.

2 Pin the pocket piece to the left side of the case inside piece, with raw edges matching at the left side and bottom. The right edge of the pocket should line up with the center line of the case inside piece. **C**

3 Baste the pocket in place, leaving the top open.

4 Apply fusible web to the remaining red spine piece 1½″ × 6″. Find and mark the lengthwise center using a fabric-safe pen.

5 Remove the paper backing from the red fabric piece.

6 With the web side down, position the red fabric piece on the gray fabric piece, matching the center fronts. Check that the spine outside and inside pieces match up. Fuse the inside spine in place.

7 Topstitch the long edges of the spine.

ASSEMBLE THE SMALL TECH CASE

1 Pin the case inside and case outside pieces right sides together.

2 Sew around the entire case using a ¼″ seam allowance. Begin 1″ from the bottom right corner of the case and stop 1″ from the bottom left corner of the case. You will have an opening approximately 6″ wide for turning.

3 Clip the corners.

4 Turn the case right side out and press well.

5 Slip the 2 pieces of 3″ × 5″ plastic canvas into the case through the opening at the bottom. Work the canvas into the outer edges of the case. You will have a piece of canvas close to each edge of the case, with the center of the case empty. **D**

6 After the canvas is in place, finger-press the case in half.

7 Press under the raw edges on the bottom of the case. Close the opening with a slip stitch.

C Pocket placement

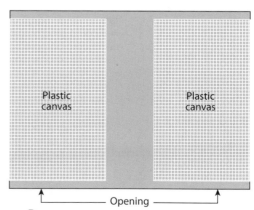

D Placement of plastic canvas inside case

Collegiate Stripe Fleece Blanket

FINISHED SIZE: 50˝ × 62˝

Any parent who has cheered on their athlete in bad weather knows it can get cold on the sidelines! Fleece blankets are a must for both watching and playing sports. This project sews up quickly and would be a great and easy gift for a teenage athlete or sports fan. Customize it with the colors of a favorite team.

Materials

- **Polar fleece for stripes and appliqué (color 1):** 1½ yards, 54″ wide

- **Polar fleece for stripes (color 2):** 1 yard, 54″ wide

- **Paper-backed fusible web:** 1 piece large enough for letter appliqué

- **Double-fold bias tape for binding:** 3 packages, ⅞″ wide

- **Thread:** to match both colors of fleece

- **Recommended sewing machine foot:** walking foot

Cutting

From polar fleece (color 1)
- 3 strips 12″ × 50″

From polar fleece (color 2)
- 3 strips 12″ × 50″

Fleece doesn't need too much pressing. However, when you do press it, make sure your iron is set for synthetics and use a pressing cloth to avoid iron shine.

Make Collegiate Stripe Blanket

ASSEMBLE THE APPLIQUÉ

Make the letter appliqué from fleece color 1, following the instructions for Using Computer Fonts as Appliqué Patterns (page 10). Use an athletic block font and make your letter 8″–10″ tall.

ASSEMBLE THE BLANKET

1 Sew the strips of fleece together along the 50″ sides, using a 1″ seam allowance. Alternate colors, starting with color 1.

2 Press the seams open.

TIP *When sewing the stripes together, be careful not to stretch the fabric. Using a walking foot on your sewing machine will be a big help.*

3 From the wrong side of the blanket, use matching thread to topstitch the raw edge of each seam allowance.

4 If needed, trim the edges of the blanket so that all edges are straight and squared.

5 Remove the paper backing from the appliqué and fuse the letter to the lower left corner of the blanket. I applied mine to the second stripe from the bottom (color 2) so that the appliqué (color 1) would stand out.

TIP *Instead of an initial, why not appliqué a jersey number instead? Or use both!*

6 Use a matching or contrasting thread to stitch around the appliqué close to the edge.

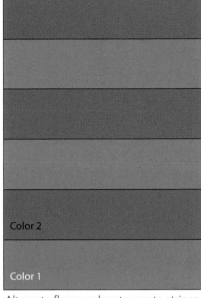

Color 2

Color 1

Alternate fleece colors to create stripes.

Fuse appliqué to front of blanket and stitch down.

BIND THE BLANKET

1 Sew the binding from all 3 packages end to end so that you have a long binding strip.

2 Lay the fleece out flat, wrong side up.

3 Unfold the binding and match the raw edge of the binding with the raw edge of the blanket. Leave 8″ of the binding unstitched when you begin sewing, and do not start at a corner. Stitch the binding in place close to the first fold in the binding.

4 To turn the corners, follow the instructions for Attach the Binding (page 18).

5 Continue stitching until you are 4″ away from where you started. Measure the binding strips so that they will match up perfectly with the blanket. Mark this point on the ends of the binding with a fabric-safe marking pen.

6 Unfold the binding and stitch the binding ends together at the marking, right sides facing each other. Trim the seam allowance to ¼″.

7 Refold the binding and finish stitching the binding to the blanket.

8 Press the binding and the seam allowance away from the blanket.

9 Bring the binding to the front of the blanket so that the folded edge just covers the stitching line. Press and pin in place. Topstitch along the edge of the binding.

Note
Use a walking foot to stitch the binding to the blanket.

THINGS TO WEAR

I remember sewing many fancy dresses for my girls when they were little. As they have grown, I've had to adjust the things I sew for them to wear. Gone are the days of frilly dresses and ribbons in their hair. It's time for something a bit more grown up.

Daddy's Girl Headbands

With their great patterns and beautiful silk fabric, neckties make wonderful headbands. Check your local thrift store or see if anyone you know has one to spare.

Materials

- **Men's necktie**
- **Grosgrain or satin ribbon:** ½ yard, 1½˝ or 2˝ wide
- **Skinny plastic headband**
- **Tools:** hot glue gun and glue

Make the Headbands

1 Measure the plastic headband end to end. Starting at the narrow end, cut the tie the same length.

2 Pin the tie piece in half lengthwise with right sides together. Create a small pleat by stitching a 1˝ line ¼˝ in from the fold, starting at the short end. Make sure to backstitch at the end of stitching line. Repeat at the other end of the tie. **A**

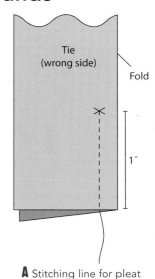

Tie
(wrong side)

Fold

1˝

A Stitching line for pleat

3 Hot glue the headband down the center of the tie, making sure to match the ends.

4 Cut a piece of ribbon 3″ long. Center the ribbon horizontally across the bottom of the headband in the center of the ribbon. **B**

5 Starting on 1 side of the inside of the headband, hot glue the ribbon to the inside of the headband. Trim off the excess ribbon. **C**

6 Fold the ribbon up onto the bottom of the headband.

7 Fold the other side of the ribbon onto the center of the headband inside. Trim the ribbon so that it extends ½″ over the side of the headband. Fold the end of the ribbon under and hot glue it into place. **D**

8 To create a clean finished edge, cut another piece of ribbon 3″. Align the finished edge of the ribbon with the bottom of the headband. Glue the ribbon to the front of the headband at the center of the ribbon. Fold the raw edges of the ribbon to the wrong side, as in Step 7, and glue in place.

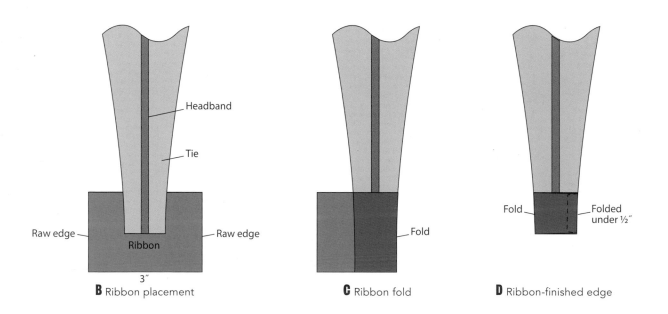

B Ribbon placement

C Ribbon fold

D Ribbon-finished edge

Chalkboard T-Shirt

Make the Chalkboard T-Shirt

1 Press the Shape-Flex onto the wrong side of the front of the T-shirt 3½˝ down from the edge of the neckband at the center front. Center the Shape-Flex on the T-shirt and make sure it's straight.

2 Apply a small amount of spray baste to the wrong side of the chalkboard vinyl piece. Place it on the right side of the T-shirt, centered over the Shape-Flex. Pin in place.

Center vinyl over Shape-Flex.

3 Using black thread and a nonstick foot on your sewing machine, stitch around the perimeter of the chalkboard vinyl piece close to the edge.

TIP *You can wash this T-shirt, but lay it flat to dry. No dryer!*

Materials

- **T-shirt of your choice**
- **Chalkboard vinyl fabric:** ¼ yard
- **Shape-Flex woven fusible interfacing:** 1 piece at least 5½˝ × 16˝
- **Basting spray**
- **Black thread**
- **Recommended sewing machine foot:** nonstick foot

Cutting

From chalkboard vinyl
- 1 piece 4˝ × 13˝

From Shape-Flex
- 1 piece 5½˝ × 16˝

Swimsuit Cover-Up

The design for this cover-up *actually started as a project for my then eight-year-old daughter. I made it and posted it on my blog and immediately got requests from readers who wanted to make an adult-sized version. It's a great, comfy summer cover-up.*

Materials

- **T-shirt A:** T-shirt in size usually worn (for example, small)
- **T-shirt B:** T-shirt 2 sizes larger (for example, large)
- **Fabric for waistband:** ¼ yard
- **Sports shoelace:** 54˝ long
- **fast2fuse fusible interfacing:** scrap at least 2˝ × 2˝
- **Thread to match waistband and T-shirt**
- **Recommended sewing machine needles and foot:** twin needle, stretch needle (designed for knit fabric), walking foot

Note

Buy men's T-shirts or non-fitted women's T-shirts. I used men's narrow-cut long T-shirts (the ones you find in the teen boys' section of the store). The shirts need to be straight and not have the curved side seams of a fitted women's shirt.

T-shirt A will be the bodice part of the cover-up; T-shirt B will form the skirt part.

Make the Swimsuit Cover-Up

All seam allowances are ½″ unless otherwise noted.

CUT THE T-SHIRTS

1 If your model is available, measure from her shoulder to her natural waist. On the front of T-shirt A, measure that distance down from the shoulder. Draw a line. Cut off the T-shirt along the line. If your model is not available, measure T-shirt A from shoulder to hem and cut off the bottom third of the shirt. **A**

2 Cut off the sleeves of T-shirt A. **A**

3 Measure 2½″ down from the center of the collar of the T-shirt. Place a mark at that point with a fabric-safe marking pen.

4 Draw a curve from the point where the collar of the T-shirt meets the shoulder seam to the mark you just made.

5 Cut the curve to the center point. **B**

6 Fold over the cut piece so that it is over the other half of the T-shirt, matching the shoulders. Trace the curve that you cut in Step 5, and finish cutting the front neckline of the T-shirt. Cutting the curve this way will help ensure that the front T-shirt neckline is symmetrical. **C**

7 On the back of the T-shirt, finish cutting off the collar.

8 Measure up 16″ from the hem of T-shirt B. Draw a line. Cut off T-shirt B along the line. Note: At this point, you can lengthen or shorten the cover-up as you like (this piece will become the skirt portion of the cover-up). **D**

A Cutting lines for T-shirt A

B Determine front neckline curve.

C Cut neckline curve on front of T-shirt.

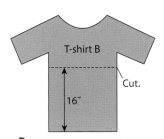

D Cutting line for T-shirt B

SEW THE T-SHIRTS

1 Install a twin needle in your sewing machine. (You may need to consult your sewing machine owner's manual to do this.) Install a walking foot on your sewing machine.

TIP *If you don't have a twin needle, just sew 2 rows of stitching about ⅛″ apart.*

2 At the neckline, fold the raw edge under ½″ and pin. Use the twin needle to stitch the neckline of the T-shirt, keeping the fold of the T-shirt even with the edge of the walking foot.

3 Hem the armholes in the same way as you hemmed the neckline in Step 2.

4 Remove the twin needle from your machine and install a stretch needle. Keep the walking foot on for the remainder of the project.

5 Stitch 2 rows of gathering stitches along the top edge of the skirt piece you cut from T-shirt B.

6 Pin the bottom of T-shirt A to the top of T-shirt B, right sides together. Adjust the gathering of T-shirt B (the skirt) to fit T-shirt A (the top). Match the centers and side seams. Stitch together.

7 Press the seam toward the top of the cover-up.

MAKE THE WAISTBAND

1 Measure around the entire waist seam, starting and ending at a side seam. Note this measurement. **E**

2 Cut the waistband fabric 3″ wide by the measurement from Step 1 plus 1″ for seam allowances.

3 Install a standard needle in your sewing machine. Sew the short ends of the waistband together. Press the seam open. Loosely pin the waistband to the waist of the cover-up to make sure it fits. Unpin.

4 Turn under each long edge of the waistband ½″ and press.

5 Find and mark the center front of the waistband.

6 Cut a 2″ × 2″ square of fast2fuse fusible interfacing. Press the square onto the wrong side of the waistband, matching the center front of the waistband and the center of the square.

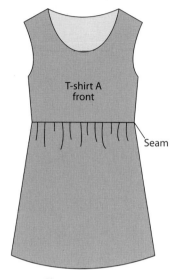

T-shirt A
front

Seam

E Measure waist.

7 Sew 2 buttonholes 15mm (about ½˝) in the center of the waistband (through the fast2fuse), 1˝ apart. **F**

8 Pin the waistband to the skirt so the bottom of the waistband just covers the seam between the 2 T-shirts. Pin well.

9 Stitch the waistband to the cover-up on the 2 long edges of the waistband. Use a thread that matches the waistband. **G**

10 Feed the shoelace through the waistband, starting at 1 buttonhole and ending at the other. Use a large safety pin to help you feed the shoelace.

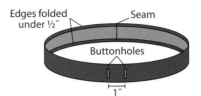

F Waistband

G Stitch waistband.

Please, Hang Up Your Towel

Materials

- **Bath towel**

- **Decorative trim:** 2 yards, 1½″ or 2″ wide

- **Fabric for appliqué:** 1 fat quarter (18″ × 22″), or scrap piece the size of your appliqué

- **Ribbon:** ⅜ yard, ¾″ wide

- **Paper-backed fusible web:** scrap piece the size of your appliqué

- **Invisible thread**

How many times have I heard, "It's not mine!" when I'm looking at a pile of wet towels on the bathroom floor. One thing I've learned raising kids is that teens are messy. The easiest way to keep things clean is to make things as simple as possible for them. I have always wondered why no one made towels with loops for hanging easily on a peg. This towel features a loop and a giant monogram so the towel owner is easily identified. No more claiming, "That's not my towel!"

Make the Towel

ASSEMBLE THE APPLIQUÉ

1 Make the initial appliqué following the instructions for Using Computer Fonts as Appliqué Patterns (page 10). I used the Museo Slab font and printed the letter 10″ tall.

2 Pin the decorative trim to the edge of the towel along the cam border (the flat accent border about 2″ in from the edge of the towel). Turn under the raw edges of the trim ¼″ on each end. Sew in place using invisible thread.

3 Repeat Step 2 for the other end of the towel.

4 Cut a piece of ribbon 10″ long.

5 Find the center of the long side of the towel and measure 3″ out from the center in both directions; mark those points.

6 Turn under the raw edges of the ribbon ½″. Pin the ribbon ends to the wrong side of the towel at the points you marked in Step 5. Align the folded ribbon ends with the edge of the towel.

7 Sew the ribbon in place close to the finished edge of the towel. Stitch over the ribbon several times to secure it. **A**

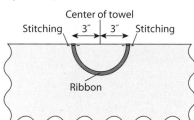

A Attach ribbon to towel.

8 Peel off the paper backing from the appliqué and center it on the towel, 4″ up from the side opposite the ribbon. Press to fuse in place.

9 Finish the edge of the appliqué with a straight stitch, following the instructions for Appliqué Stitching (page 12). Use a thread color that matches your appliqué or the towel.

Sew appliqué to towel using straight stitch.

STUFF FOR THEIR ROOMS

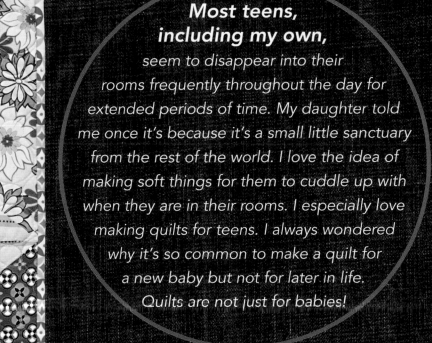

Most teens, including my own, seem to disappear into their rooms frequently throughout the day for extended periods of time. My daughter told me once it's because it's a small little sanctuary from the rest of the world. I love the idea of making soft things for them to cuddle up with when they are in their rooms. I especially love making quilts for teens. I always wondered why it's so common to make a quilt for a new baby but not for later in life. Quilts are not just for babies!

Everything's Coming Up Posies Quilt

FINISHED SIZE: 59½″ × 59½″ (not including binding)

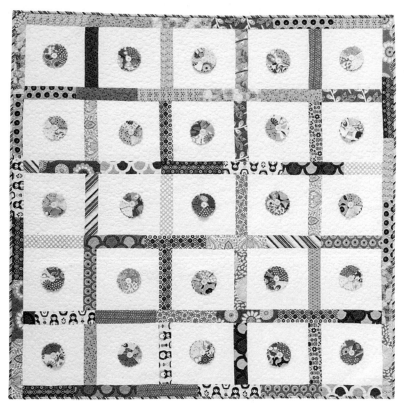

Pieced by:
Melissa Mortenson

Quilted by:
Natalia Bonner

Fabric:
Sugar Pop by Moda and
Little Matryoshka by Riley Blake

Materials

- **White fabric for blocks:** 25 white layer cake squares (10″ × 10″ each), or 2¼ yards

- **Fabric for sashing:** 40 jelly roll strips (2½″ × 42″ each)

- **Print fabric for flowers:** 100 charm squares (5″ × 5″ each)

- **White fabric for backing:** 2½ yards

- **Print fabric for backing:** ⅓ yard each of 6 different prints (2 yards total)

- **Fabric for binding:** ½ yard

- **Batting:** 1 piece 67″ × 67″ (Join 2 pieces if necessary.)

- **Buttons:** 25, approximately 1″ diameter

Cutting

Refer to Flower pattern (page 100).

From fabric roll for sashing
- 76 pieces 2½″ × 10″

From white fabric for blocks (if not using precuts)
- 25 pieces 10″ × 10″

From precut squares 5″ × 5″
- 100 flowers using the Flower pattern (page 100)

From white fabric for backing
- 6 pieces 12″ × 34″

From print fabrics for backing
- 6 pieces 12″ × 34″

From binding fabric
- 7 strips 2½″ × 40″

Make the Quilt

ASSEMBLE THE ROWS

All seam allowances are ¼″ unless otherwise noted.

1 Sew 1 strip 2½″ × 10″ to 1 white square 10″ × 10″. **A**

2 Sew a second white square to the other side of the same strip. Repeat until the entire row is complete, ending with a white square. Press the seams to 1 side. You will have 5 squares and 4 sashing strips in the row. **B**

3 Repeat Steps 1 and 2 to make a total of 5 rows. Each row should measure 56″. Label the rows 1 through 5.

ASSEMBLE THE SASHING

1 Sew 7 pieces 2½″ × 10″ together along the short ends. Press the seams to 1 side. Repeat until you have 6 pieced strips, each made from 7 pieces. These are the sashing strips.

2 Sew a sashing strip to the top of row 1, right sides facing. Trim the strip to match the row. Press the seams to 1 side.

3 Sew the second sashing strip to the bottom of row 1, with right sides facing and staggering the seams. You will have extra sashing on either or both ends. Trim to match the length of row 1. Press the seams to 1 side. **C**

4 Sew the top of row 2 to the bottom of the second sashing strip.

5 Repeat Steps 3 and 4, staggering the seams of each sashing strip, until all 5 rows are sewn together with the 6 sashing strips. **D**

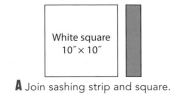

A Join sashing strip and square.

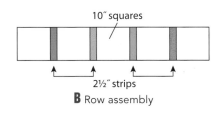

10″ squares

2½″ strips

B Row assembly

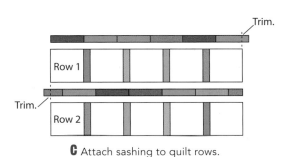

Trim.

Row 1

Trim.

Row 2

C Attach sashing to quilt rows.

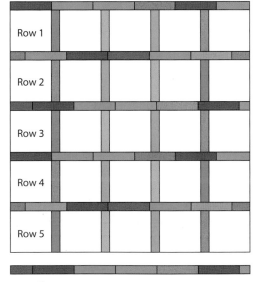

Row 1

Row 2

Row 3

Row 4

Row 5

D Alternate rows and pieced sashing.

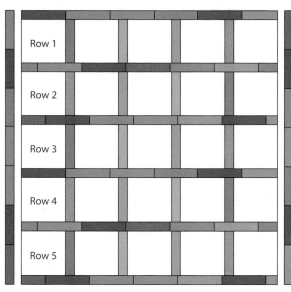

Row 1

Row 2

Row 3

Row 4

Row 5

E Attach pieced borders.

SEW THE BORDERS

1 Sew 7 strips 2½″ × 10″ together along the short ends. Press the seams to 1 side. Repeat to create another long strip.

2 Measure the right and left sides of the quilt (the sides that have no sashing). Determine an average if the 2 sides are not the same.

3 Mark that measurement on the 2 border strips.

4 Pin border strips to each side of the quilt top, right sides facing. Line up the marked measurements on the border with the edges of the quilt top.

5 Stitch the border strips to the quilt. Trim the borders to match the edges of the quilt. **E**

MAKE THE FLOWERS

1 Fold 3 flower pieces in half with wrong sides together. Press. **F**

2 Fold each piece again—this time fold over one third at 1 of the corners. Press. **G**

3 Layer all 3 of the folded flowers on top of an unfolded flower piece. Stitch a square shape in the center of the flower to attach all the layers together. **H**

4 Repeat Steps 1–3 to make a total of 25 flowers. Set aside.

F Fold flower piece in half.

G Fold over one third at corner.

H Layer 3 flower pieces and stitch together.

MAKE THE QUILT BACK

1. Sew together a white backing piece 12″ × 34″ and a printed backing piece 12″ × 34″ along the long side, using a ½″ seam allowance. Press the seam open.

2. Repeat Step 1 to sew 4 more pieces together, alternating white and print fabrics. You will have a total of 6 pieces in the section.

3. Repeat Steps 1 and 2 to create another section of 6 alternating pieces.

4. Sew together the 2 sections of the quilt back along the long edge, matching seams and alternating white and print fabrics. Press the center seam open. The backing should measure 67″ × 67″. **I**

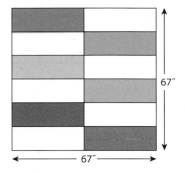

I Quilt backing layout

FINISH THE QUILT

1. Layer, quilt, and bind as desired (see Quiltmaking Basics, page 17).

2. Pin a sewn flower onto the center of a white square. Center a button on top of the flower. Stitch the button and the flower to the quilt. Repeat for all 25 flowers. **J**

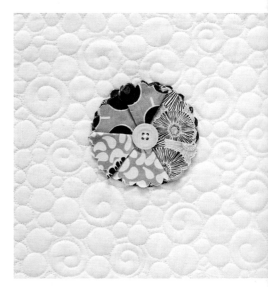

J Attach flowers to quilt top.

Everything's Coming Up Posies Quilt
Flower pattern

Diamonds Are a Girl's Best Friend Quilt

FINISHED SIZE: 50¼″ × 60½″

Pieced by:
Melissa Mortenson

Quilted by:
Natalia Bonner

Fabrics:
Meadowsweet by Sandi Henderson

Materials

- **Fabric for quilt blocks:** 15 fat quarters (18″ × 22″ each) in a variety of prints
- **Flannel for quilt backing:** 3½ yards
- **Fabric for binding:** ½ yard
- **Batting:** 1 piece 59″ × 69″ (Join 2 pieces if necessary.)

Cutting

From fat quarters for blocks

- 15 pieces 13″ × 18″

From flannel for backing

- 2 pieces 63″ × width of fabric

From binding fabric

- 7 pieces 2½″ × 40″

Make the Quilt

CUT AND ARRANGE THE DIAMONDS

Handle the cut triangles as little as possible. Pieces cut on the diagonal stretch easily.

1 Cut each piece 13″ × 18″ diagonally. **A**

2 *Without moving the fabric*, cut each piece again along the other diagonal. **B**

3 You now have 4 triangles of each print, but with 2 different dimensions. These are now referred to as *triangles A and B.*

4 Arrange the quilt pieces on a flat surface or design wall. Refer to the quilt layout (page 104) for placement. Matching colors indicate fabrics of the same print.

Note
For this quilt, it is very important that you arrange all the pieces in order before you start sewing.

A Cut rectangle diagonally.

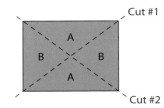

B Cut second diagonal to create triangles A and B.

ASSEMBLE THE BLOCKS

1 Starting in the upper left corner, sew 1 triangle A to 1 triangle B. Press the seam toward triangle B. **C**

2 Sew the other pair of A and B triangles together. Press seam toward triangle B.

3 Sew the 2 sets of paired triangles together along the diagonal edge. Press the seam to 1 side. This makes 1 rectangular block. **D**

4 Repeat Steps 1–3 until you have 15 blocks. Remember to sew the blocks together according to your layout to ensure that the correct prints are next to each other.

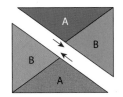

C Sew triangles A and B together.

D Complete block by sewing together pairs of triangles.

ASSEMBLE THE QUILT TOP

1 Sew together the blocks by rows. There are 3 blocks in each of the 5 rows. Refer to the quilt layout (at right).

2 Sew the rows together and press the seams to 1 side.

MAKE THE QUILT BACK

1 Cut the backing fabric into 2 equal lengths (1¾ yards each). Trim the selvage from 1 side of each piece.

2 Sew together the 2 trimmed edges, right sides facing, using a ½˝ seam allowance. Press the seam open.

3 With the seam positioned *horizontally* (parallel to the top and bottom of the quilt top), trim the backing to 59˝ wide × 69˝ long.

FINISH THE QUILT

Layer, quilt, and bind as desired (see Quiltmaking Basics, page 17).

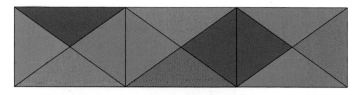

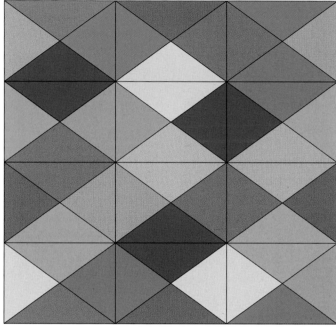

Quilt layout

Study Pillow

FINISHED SIZE: Standard size bed pillow (19˝ × 26˝)

One day I saw my daughter headed outside to study. She had in her hand a pillow, a bunch of books, some notebooks, and her iPod. As she struggled to get all the items outside, I remember thinking, "Wouldn't it be easier if she had pockets on her pillow?" Hence, the study pillow was born! It's super soft on one side (for a little study-break nap!) and the other side has pockets for things like notebooks and pencils. It also has a handle to make it easy to carry around.

Materials

- **Fabric for pillow front:** ¾ yard
- **Minky fabric (microfiber chenille) for pillow back:** ¾ yard
- **Fabric for large pocket:** 1 fat quarter (18″ × 22″)
- **Fabric for large pocket lining:** 1 fat quarter
- **Fabric for small pocket and lining:** 1 fat quarter
- **Fabric for pillow side panel:** 1 fat quarter
- **Fabric for appliqué:** scrap piece about 9″ × 12″
- **Fusible fleece:** ¾ yard
- **Paper-backed fusible web for appliqué:** scrap piece about 9″ × 11″
- **Decorative ribbon:** ½ yard, ⅝″–1″ wide
- **Piping:** 1 package premade, or 2¾ yards
- **Pillow form:** standard bed pillow, 19″ × 26″

Cutting

From fat quarters

- 1 piece 13″ × 18″ for large pocket front
- 1 piece 13″ × 18″ for large pocket lining
- 1 piece 9″ × 19″ for side panel
- 1 piece 7″ × 7″ for small pocket
- 1 piece 7″ × 7″ for small pocket lining

From pillow front fabric

- 1 piece 18″ × 19″

TIP *You may want to fussy cut the small pocket piece, which means to select a specific section of the print to cut.*

From Minky fabric

- 1 piece 17″ × 19″ for pillow back

From fusible fleece

- 1 piece 13″ × 18″

A Fuse and sew appliqué to bottom right corner.

Make the Study Pillow

All seam allowances are ½˝ unless otherwise stated.

MAKE THE LARGE POCKET

1 Make the "study" appliqué following the instructions for Using Computer Fonts as Appliqué Patterns (page 10). I used Pacifico font, and the word is 8˝ long.

2 Fuse the appliqué piece to the large pocket piece 1½˝ from the bottom right corner. Stitch through the center of the appliqué piece to secure. **A**

3 Apply fusible fleece to the back of the large pocket piece 13˝ × 18˝.

4 Attach piping to the top edge of the large pocket piece, following the instructions for Working with Piping (page 14).

5 Pin the large pocket front to the large pocket lining, right sides facing. Sew the pocket pieces together along the top, using the stitching line you created when attaching the piping as a guide.

6 Turn right side out and press.

7 Baste together the 3 remaining sides of the large pocket piece, matching raw edges. Set the pocket aside.

Large pocket attached to pillow front

MAKE THE SMALL POCKET

1 Pin the small pocket front to the small pocket lining, right sides facing. Sew together using a ¼" seam. Leave a 2" opening in the bottom of the pocket.

2 Clip the corners, turn the pocket right side out, and press. Turn in the raw edges at the bottom of the pocket, and press.

3 Topstitch along the upper edge of the pocket piece. Set the pocket aside.

MAKE THE PILLOW FRONT

1 Pin the large pocket piece to the pillow front piece 18" × 19", matching the 18" sides. Baste in place. **B**

2 Pin the side panel 9" × 19" to the left side of the pillow front piece. Stitch together using a ⅜" seam. Press the seam open.

3 Pin the small pocket to the side panel, about 4" down from the top and centered. **C**

4 Sew the small pocket in place along the side and bottom seams.

5 Attach piping to the outside edge of the completed pillow front piece, following the instructions for Working with Piping (page 14).

Small pocket attached to pillow front

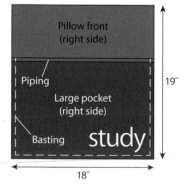

B Pin large pocket to pillow front.

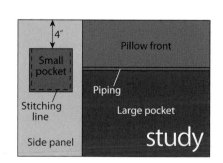

C Pillow front layout

ASSEMBLE THE STUDY PILLOW

1 Cut a piece of ribbon 14″ long.

2 Find the center of the top edge of the pillow front and measure 3″ out from the center in both directions; mark those points.

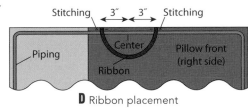

3 Pin the ribbon ends to the pillow front at the 2 marked points. Sew in place near the edge. **D**

D Ribbon placement

4 Pin the pillow front to the pillow back, right sides facing. Sew together with the pillow front on top, using the stitching line you created when attaching the piping as a guide. Leave an opening about 20″ wide on the bottom edge.

TIP *When sewing stretchy fabric (such as Minky chenille) to woven fabric, place the stretchy fabric on the bottom. The feed dogs of your machine will help evenly feed the stretchy fabric.*

5 Clip the corners. Turn the pillow right side out.

6 Insert the pillow form into the pillow. Slipstitch the opening closed.

You Can Do It Quilt

FINISHED SIZE: 54˝ × 54˝

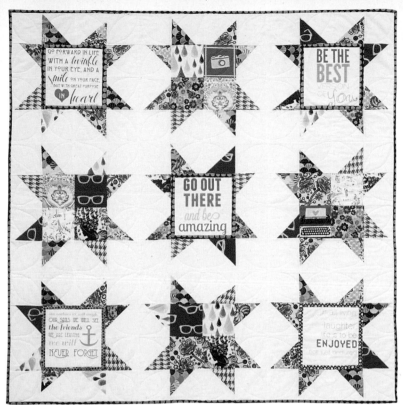

> **I try to make** a quilt for each of my nieces and nephews when they head off to college. My sister-in-law gave me the idea of incorporating some inspirational quotes into the blocks of this one. I think it makes a fun gift.

Pieced and quilted by:
Melissa Mortenson

Materials

- **Fabric for nonquote blocks:** ½ yard total, various prints

- **Fabric for wonky triangles:** 1 yard total, various prints

- **White fabric:** 108 charm squares (5″ × 5″), or 2⅛ yards

- **Fabric for quote borders:** 1 fat quarter (18″ × 22″) for all the borders, or up to 5 different prints, each about 4″ × 11″

- **Printable fabric sheets:** 5, at least 8½″ × 11″

- **Fabric for backing:** 1 yard each of 4 different prints

- **Fabric for binding:** ½ yard

- **Batting:** 60″ × 60″ piece (Join 2 pieces if necessary.)

TIP *The print fabrics are cut into 5″ × 5″ squares or short 1¼″ strips, so this is a great way to use up some of your stash! You can even mix it up and use multiple prints in the border for a single quote.*

Cutting

From fabric for nonquote blocks
- 16 pieces 5″ × 5″ from various prints

From fabric for wonky triangles
- 36 pieces 5″ × 5″ from various prints

From fat quarters for quote block borders
- 10 pieces 1¼″ × 9½″
- 10 pieces 1¼″ × 8″

TIP *If you are using a different print for each border, make sure you cut 2 pieces of each size from each fat quarter.*

From white fabric (if not using precut squares)
- 14 strips 5″ each

  Subcut each strip into 8 squares 5″ × 5″. You will have a total of 112 squares.

From fabric for backing
- 4 pieces 31½″ × 31½″ (1 from each print)

From binding fabric
- 6 strips 2½″ × 40″

Make the Quilt

All seam allowances are ¼″ unless otherwise noted.

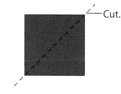

A Make Four-Patch square for center of block A.

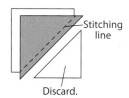

B Cut 5″ square diagonally into 2 triangles.

ASSEMBLE THE PATCHED CENTERS FOR BLOCK A

1 Sew together 2 squares 5″ × 5″ of print fabric along a side. Press the seam to 1 side.

2 Sew together 2 more squares 5″ × 5″ along a side. Press the seam in the opposite direction.

3 Sew the 2 pairs from Steps 1 and 2 together to form a Four-Patch square. Press the seam to 1 side. **A**

4 Repeat Steps 1–3 to make a total of 4 blocks. These are the center units for block A. The Four-Patch should measure 9½″ × 9½″. Trim if necessary.

CONSTRUCT THE WONKY HALF-SQUARE TRIANGLES

C Sew triangle onto white square.

D Trim off extra white fabric.

1 Cut each of the 36 squares 5″ × 5″ in half diagonally to make 72 triangles. **B**

2 Pin a cut triangle diagonally across a white square 5″ × 5″, right sides facing. The exact location is up to you, but check that when you flip up the triangle, it extends past the edges of the white square. Sew in place. **C**

TIP *When sewing the triangles onto the white squares, vary the placement of the triangles to alter the angles. Before you stitch in place, remember to check that when you flip up the triangle, it extends past the edges of the white square.*

3 Cut off the extra white fabric, leaving ¼″ seam allowance. **D**

4 Flip up the triangle and press the seam to 1 side.

5 Trim the completed wonky half-square triangle so that it is a 5″ square. **E**

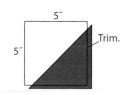

E Trim wonky half-square triangles.

6 Repeat Steps 2–5 until you have completed 72 wonky half-square triangles.

ASSEMBLE THE QUOTE CENTERS FOR BLOCK B

1 Create your own inspirational quotes to print or download mine in PDF format from polkadotchair.com/book. Print quotes onto printable fabric sheets. Follow the manufacturer's instructions for treating the fabric after it is printed.

2 Make 5 printed quotes.

3 Trim the printed sheets to 8″ × 8″ squares.

4 Sew 1 strip 1¼″ × 8″ to the top of a printed square. Sew another strip 1¼″ × 8″ to the bottom of the square. Press the seams away from the center of the square.

5 Sew 1 strip 1¼″ × 9½″ to each of the 2 remaining sides of the printed square. Press the seams away from the center of the block. **F**

6 Repeat Steps 4 and 5 until you have 5 completed quote block centers. These are the centers of block B. Each block center should measure 9½″ × 9½″. Trim if needed.

CONSTRUCT BLOCK A

Refer to the block A assembly diagram (below) for placement of half-square triangles.

1 Assemble the top row by sewing a white square 5″ × 5″ to a wonky half-square triangle. Sew another half-square triangle to the other side. Finish the row by sewing a white square 5″ × 5″ next to the second half-square triangle.

2 Assemble the bottom row by repeating Step 1, except that the triangles should point in the opposite direction.

3 Sew together 2 half-square triangles for each side.

4 Sew the half-square triangle pairs to the right and left sides of the Four-Patch center piece, matching seams.

5 Press the seams to 1 side.

6 Sew the top row from Step 1 to top of the center piece, matching seams.

7 Sew the bottom row from Step 2 to the bottom of the center piece, matching seams. **G**

8 Press all of the seams to 1 side. Trim any uneven edges.

9 Repeat Steps 1–8 to make a total of 4 block A's.

CONSTRUCT BLOCK B

Refer to the block B assembly diagram (below) for placement of half-square triangles.

1 Follow Steps 1–8 of Construct Block A (above) to make block B, using a printed quote as the center. **H**

2 Repeat Step 1 to make a total of 5 block B's.

F Assemble quote blocks.

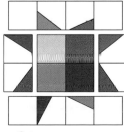

G Block A assembly

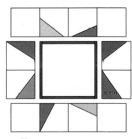

H Block B assembly

ASSEMBLE THE QUILT

1 Sew blocks together by rows, using the quilt layout diagram for reference. Press all the seams to 1 side. **I**

2 Sew the rows of the quilt together. Press all the seams to 1 side.

MAKE THE QUILT BACK

1 Sew together 2 quilt back pieces 31½˝ × 31½˝ using a ½˝ seam allowance. Press the seam open.

2 Sew together the other 2 quilt back pieces 31½˝ × 31½˝ with a ½˝ seam allowance. Press the seam open.

3 Sew together the 2 pairs of quilt back pieces, matching the center seams and using a ½˝ seam allowance. Press the seam open. **J**

FINISH THE QUILT

Layer, quilt, and bind as desired (see Quiltmaking Basics, page 17).

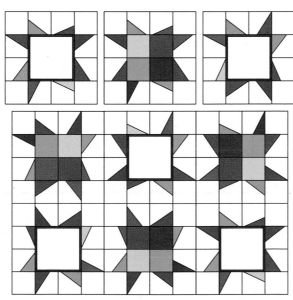

I Quilt layout

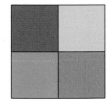

J Quilt backing layout

DREAM

Quatrefoil Quilt

FINISHED SIZE: 51″ × 68″

A few years ago, our family visited Istanbul. I loved the unique geometric patterns that were everywhere, especially on the tiles in the Blue Mosque. Since my visit, I thought it would be fun to mimic the look of the tiles in a quilt using shades of pink instead of blue. Perfect for a teenage girl.

Pieced by:
Melissa Mortenson

Quilted by:
Natalia Bonner and Melissa Mortenson

Fabrics:
Kona Cotton Solids

Materials

- **Pink fabrics for squares:** 3¼ yards
  (Each piece must be at least ¼ yard. I used 13 different shades of Kona Cottons pink.)
- **White fabric for quatrefoil shapes:** 2½ yards
- **Paper-backed fusible web:** 5¼ yards, 17″ wide
- **Fabric for backing:** 3½ yards
- **Fabric for binding:** ⅝ yard
- **Batting:** 1 piece 59″ × 76″
  (Join 2 smaller pieces if necessary.)

Cutting

From pink fabrics
- 48 squares 9″ × 9″

From white fabric
- 48 squares 8″ × 8″

From binding fabric
- 7 strips 2½″ × width of fabric

Make the Quilt

All seam allowances are ¼″ unless otherwise noted.

CREATE THE APPLIQUÉ PIECES

1 Trace the Quatrefoil pattern (page 119) onto a piece of sturdy paper to make a template. I like to use inkjet photo paper. This template is used for tracing all of the quatrefoil shapes.

2 Using your template, trace 48 quatrefoil shapes onto the paper side of the paper-backed fusible web.

3 Roughly cut out around each shape.

4 With the paper side up, press each of the 48 shapes onto a white square 8″ × 8″. **A**

5 Precisely cut out all of the quatrefoil shapes from the white fabric.

6 Peel off the paper backing and turn the shape fabric side up. Place each onto a pink square 9″ × 9″. Make sure the quatrefoil shapes are perfectly centered on the pink squares. Press into place.

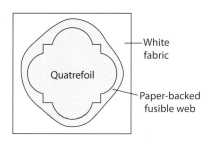

White fabric

Quatrefoil

Paper-backed fusible web

A Press quatrefoil shape onto white fabric.

TIP *To ensure that all of your quatrefoil shapes are properly centered on your blocks, cut a piece of cardstock 9″ × 9″ and then cut a 7″ × 7″ hole from its center. Place this frame on top of each pink square, with all outside edges matching. Place a quatrefoil shape just inside the edges.*

7 Finish the edges of the appliqués with a blanket stitch, following the instructions for Appliqué Stitching (page 12).

ASSEMBLE THE QUILT TOP

1 Sew together a row of 6 blocks 9″ × 9″. Avoid placing any 2 blocks in the same shade of pink next to each other. Press seams to 1 side.

2 Repeat Step 1 for all 8 of the rows.

3 Sew the rows together. Press seams to 1 side.

MAKE THE QUILT BACK

1 Cut the backing fabric into 2 equal lengths (1¾ yards each). Trim the selvage from a side of each piece.

2 Sew together the 2 trimmed edges, right sides facing, using a ½″ seam allowance. Press the seam open.

3 With the seam positioned horizontally (parallel to the top and bottom), trim the backing to 59″ wide × 76″ long.

FINISH THE QUILT

Layer, quilt, and bind as desired (see Quiltmaking Basics, page 17).

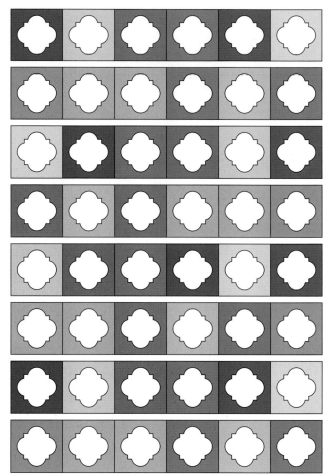

Quilt layout

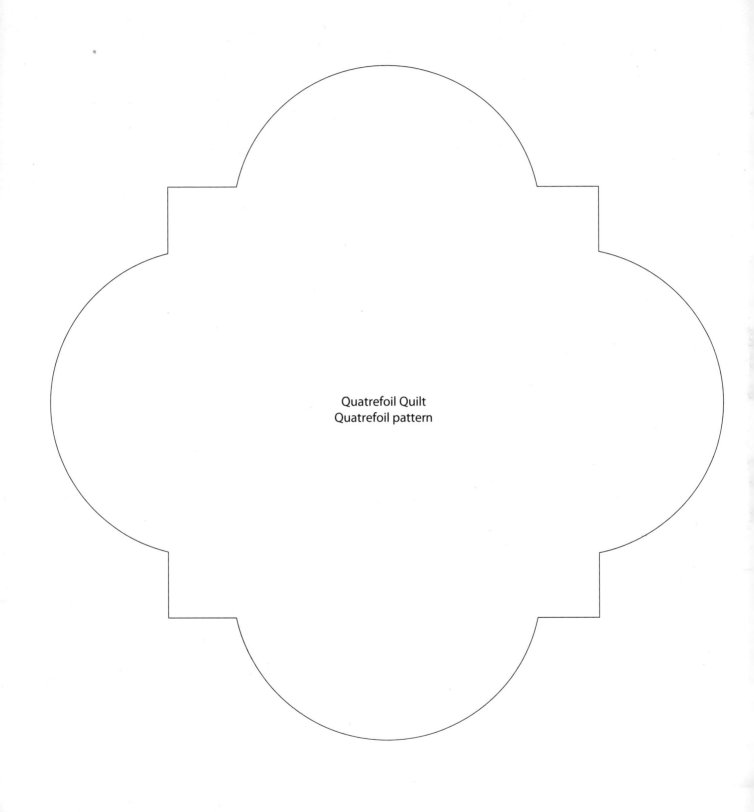

Quatrefoil Quilt
Quatrefoil pattern

Pocket-ful Quilt

FINISHED SIZE: 55″ × 66″

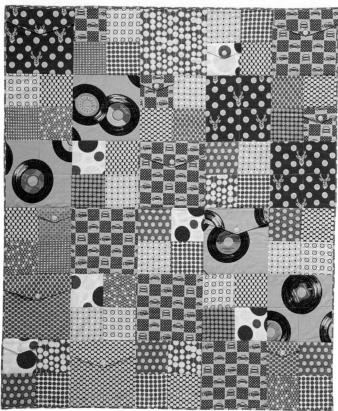

Quilted and pieced by:
Melissa Mortenson

Materials

- **Fabrics for large blocks:** 2 yards total, in ⅓-yard cuts of up to 6 different prints

- **Fabrics for large pockets and linings:** 2 yards total, in ⅓-yard cuts of up to 6 different prints

- **Fabrics for small blocks:** 2 yards total, in ⅓-yard cuts of up to 6 different prints

- **Fabrics for small pockets and linings:** ¾ yard total in a variety of prints

- **Fusible fleece:** 1 yard, 45″ wide

- **Fabric for backing:** 4 yards

- **Fabric for binding:** ½ yard

- **Batting:** 1 piece 63″ × 74″

- **Buttons:** 1″ size, or various sizes of your choice

TIPS *This quilt takes some detailed planning and perhaps auditioning of fabrics for the different blocks and pockets. You can make a quilt with an entirely different "look" than the one I made. Plus, this quilt is a great one for a boy—just use plaids, stripes, and solids in his favorite color palette.*

● *The pocket front and pocket flap pieces should be cut from the same fabric. For the small pockets and linings, you could use leftover pieces from the large pockets and their linings, or you can use scraps from other projects. Linings don't have to match; use any coordinating or contrasting fabrics from your stash. Put some surprise colors in those pockets!*

Cutting

Refer to Pocket Flap patterns (page 126).

From fabric for large blocks
- 15 squares 11½″ × 11½″

From fabric for large pockets and pocket flaps
- 6 pieces 9″ × 11½″ for pocket fronts
- 6 pieces from Large Pocket Flap pattern

From fabric for large pocket lining
- 6 pieces 9″ × 11½″ for pocket fronts
- 6 pieces from Large Pocket Flap pattern

From fabric for small blocks
- 60 squares 6″ × 6″

From fabric for small pockets
- 6 pieces 5″ × 6″ for pocket fronts
- 6 pieces from Small Pocket Flap pattern

From fabric for small pocket lining
- 6 pieces 5″ × 6″ for pocket fronts
- 6 pieces from the Small Pocket Flap pattern

From fusible fleece
- 6 pieces 9″ × 11½″
- 6 pieces 5″ × 6″
- 6 pieces from Large Pocket Flap pattern
- 6 pieces from Small Pocket Flap pattern

From binding fabric
- 7 strips 2½″ × width of fabric

Make the Quilt
All seam allowances are ¼″ unless otherwise noted.

MAKE THE POCKET BLOCKS

1 Apply fusible fleece to the wrong side of the 6 large pocket fronts 9″ × 11½″ and the 6 small pocket fronts 5″ × 6″.

2 Pin a pocket lining piece to a fused pocket piece, right sides together. Stitch along the top edge.

3 Press the seam open.

4 Turn the pocket piece right side up and press flat. Topstitch along the seam on the lining side.

5 Fold the pocket piece along the seamline and press.

6 Repeat Steps 2–5 for all 12 pockets, matching large pockets to large linings and small pockets to small linings.

7 Baste each large lined pocket piece to a large square 11½″ × 11½″, lining up the raw edges on the sides and bottom. The pocket fabric does not need to match the block fabric. These sewn pieces are now referred to as the *large pocket blocks*. **A**

8 Baste each small lined pocket piece to a small square 6″ × 6″, lining up the raw edges on the sides and bottom. The pocket fabric does not need to match the block fabric. These sewn pieces are now referred to as the *small pocket blocks*. **B**

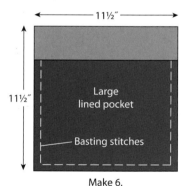

Make 6.

A Large pocket block

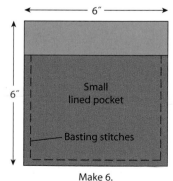

Make 6.

B Small pocket block

MAKE THE NONPOCKET PAIRS

1 Sew together 2 of the small block pieces 6″ × 6″ along a side. If your print has an up-and-down pattern, make sure both squares are facing the same direction. Try not to place 2 of the same print next to each other. Press the seams to 1 side.

2 These sewn pieces are now referred to as *nonpocket pairs*. Repeat Step 1 to make 24. **C**

MAKE THE POCKET PAIRS

1 Sew together 1 small pocket block and 1 square 6″ × 6″ along a side. Press the seam to 1 side. Refer to the quilt layout diagram (page 124) to see where these blocks will be placed.

2 Each of these sewn pieces is a *pocket pair*. Repeat Step 1 to make a total of 6, following the pocket pair assembly diagrams. **D**

3 Sew together a nonpocket pair and a pocket pair to form a square. Press the seam to 1 side. This piece is now referred to as *block B*. Make 6, following the block B assembly diagrams. **E**

4 Sew together 2 sets of nonpocket pairs to make a Four-Patch block. Press the seam to 1 side. This piece is now referred to as *block A*. Make 9. **F**

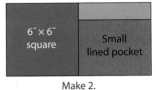

Make 24.

C Nonpocket pairs

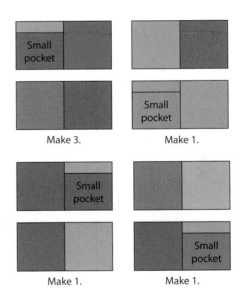

Make 4.　　　　Make 2.

D Pocket pair assembly

Make 3.　　　　Make 1.

Make 1.　　　　Make 1.

E Block B assembly

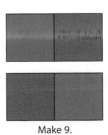

Make 9.

F Block A assembly

MAKE THE POCKET FLAPS

1 Apply fusible fleece to the wrong side of the 6 large pocket flap pieces.

2 Pin a large pocket flap lining piece to the fused large pocket flap piece, with right sides facing. Stitch all around, leaving a 3″ opening in the top of the flap.

3 Clip the corners, turn right side, out and press.

4 Turn the raw edges in at the top of the pocket flap and press. Baste the top of the pocket flap closed.

5 Topstitch the pocket flap along the sides and bottom. **G**

6 Sew a vertical buttonhole in the center of each pocket flap. Be sure to make the buttonhole the correct size to fit the button you've selected.

7 Repeat Steps 2–6 to make a total of 6 large pocket flaps.

8 Repeat Steps 1–6 to make 6 small pocket flaps.

ASSEMBLE THE QUILT TOP

1 Sew blocks together by rows using the quilt layout diagram (at right) as a guide. Press all the seams to 1 side.

2 Sew rows 1–6 together. Press all the seams to 1 side.

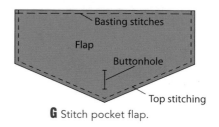

G Stitch pocket flap.

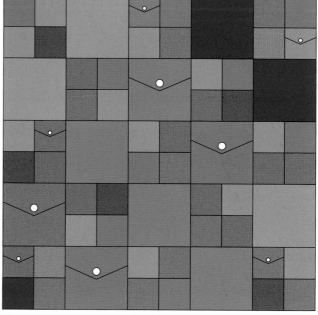

Quilt layout

MAKE THE QUILT BACK

1 Cut the backing fabric into 2 equal lengths (2 yards each). Trim the selvage from 1 side of each piece.

2 Sew together the 2 trimmed edges, right sides facing, using a ½″ seam allowance. Press the seam open.

3 With the seam positioned horizontally (parallel to the top and bottom of the quilt top), trim the backing to 63″ wide × 74″ long.

FINISH THE QUILT

Layer, quilt, and bind as desired (see Quiltmaking Basics, page 17).

Note
Be careful not to quilt over any of the pockets!

ATTACH THE POCKET FLAPS

1 Pin the pocket flap to the corresponding pocket on the quilt. Stitch the pocket flap to the quilt along the top edge of the flap, sewing through all of the layers. **H**

2 Repeat Step 1 for all 6 large pocket blocks and 6 small pocket blocks.

3 Sew buttons onto the pockets.

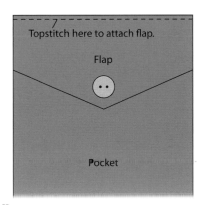

Topstitch here to attach flap.

Flap

Pocket

H Attach pocket flaps to completed quilt.

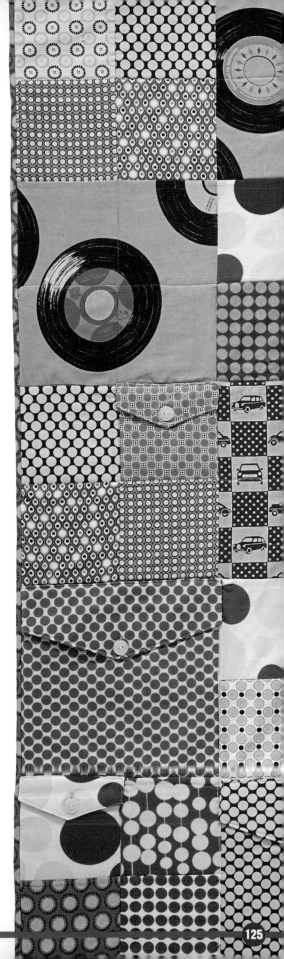

Pocket-ful Quilt
Small Pocket Flap pattern

Pocket-ful Quilt
Large Pocket Flap pattern

Place on fabric fold.

SUPPLIES AND RESOURCES

The first place to go for information and products is your local quilt shop or craft store. If that is not possible or they cannot help you, try the Internet resources listed here.

Sewing Machines and Accessories

Bernina www.bernina.com

Manufacturers and Designers of the Fabrics Used in This Book

Riley Blake Designs rileyblakedesigns.com

Robert Kaufman, Kona Cotton Solids
robertkaufman.com/fabrics/kona_cotton

Moda Fabrics unitednotions.com

Birch Fabrics birchfabrics.com

Echino sevenislandsfabric.com

Melody Miller melodymiller.net

Tula Pink tulapink.com

Heather Bailey heatherbailey.com

Amy Butler amybutlerdesign.com

Machine Quilting Services

Natalia Bonner piecenquilt.com

Fonts (mostly free)

dafont.com

fontsquirrel.com

fontspace.com

losttype.com (nominal fee for Wisdom Script)

Other Supplies

Aurifil thread www.aurifil.com

Therm O Web iron-on vinyl
thermowebonline.com

Printable cotton fabric
The Electric Quilt Company electricquilt.com

Lesley Riley's TAP Transfer Artist Paper, Alex Anderson's 4-in-1 Essential Sewing Tool, and various interfacings
C&T Publishing ctpub.com

About the Author

Melissa Mortenson lives in Louisville, Kentucky, with her husband and three teenagers. She is the author of the Polka Dot Chair blog (polkadotchair.com), where she has been sharing creative ideas with readers for six years. She loves to sew, cook, eat, and leave town whenever possible.

Connect with Melissa:

Blog polkadotchair.com

Facebook facebook.com/ThePolkaDotChair

Pinterest pinterest.com/PolkaDotChair

Twitter @Polkadotchair

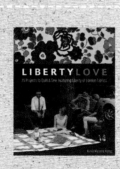